"Perfectionists, procrastinators, and people-pleasers take note. There is a new book available that can change how you live your life! *The CBT Workbook for Perfectionism* by Sharon Martin is more than a book; it's a program. If you find yourself caught up in self-criticism and self-judgment, struggling with deadlines, or sabotaging your own success, you will find enormous comfort and guidance in this well-thought-out, highly structured workbook."

—**Jonice Webb, PhD,** nationally recognized pioneer in the area of
childhood emotional neglect, and best-selling author of *Running on Empty*
and *Running on Empty No More*

"This workbook redefines what it means to work through your stuff. It's chock-full of activities that help you really think about what you want to change AND gets you actively moving towards the change you want to see. The workbook takes you from understanding perfectionism to navigating the tough road to recovering from perfectionism to being able to live a life without the guilt and people-pleasing that come from being a perfectionist. And while many workbooks claim to do this, the way Sharon has crafted this workbook shows you step by practical step how to succeed at making this a solid transition. Professionals will love working with this book in their practices, and clients will love working through their perfectionism with such a useful guide."

—**Mercedes Samudio, LCSW,** parent coach, and best-selling author of
Shame-Proof Parenting

T0385211

"I'm a big fan of workbooks because they allow the reader to become an active participant in their self-help efforts. Sharon Martin's contribution to help people fight perfectionism is a fantastic antidote to getting perfectionism's maladaptive behaviors better under control. Martin offers a direct and no-nonsense look at perfectionism that eschews psychobabble, pulling together techniques in a cohesive and sensible manner. This workbook works well as either an adjunct to psychotherapy, or as a stand-alone guide to those in need of help of silencing the perfectionist in themselves. There's no better book on the market that offers such practical advice and exercises for someone who wants better control over their perfectionism."

—**John M. Grohol, PsyD,** founder and editor-in-chief of www.psychcentral.com

"Many people struggle with perfectionism whether it's in our workplaces, in relationships, or the battle within ourselves. And many books talk about its root causes and how perfectionism affects the human psyche. But rarely do books offer ways to address perfectionism. In *The CBT Workbook for Perfectionism*, Sharon Martin offers practical, concrete, research-driven ways to let go of struggles like self-criticism, procrastination, people-pleasing, and the need for control. A must-read for anyone whose potential has been hindered by perfectionism."

—**Melvin Varghese, PhD**, psychologist, and founder of Selling The Couch

"Perfectionism can be paralyzing, but Sharon Martin gives you a road map to reclaim your life. Sharon expertly guides you to down a path to self-discovery, and arms you with exercises to find mental and emotional freedom. For lifelong high achievers, *The CBT Workbook for Perfectionism* is a must-have companion that will help you embrace imperfect action and reach your goals with less stress."

—**Melody Wilding, LMSW**, peak performance coach, and adjunct professor
of human behavior at The City University of New York

"Sharon Martin has been a trusted resource for my clinical work for years. She has a way of breaking down complex topics into understandable explanations, which makes them easier to understand and address. This workbook is no exception. She clearly explains what perfectionism is, how it shows up in our lives, where it comes from, and what we can do to change the perfectionistic behavior, which can be so problematic in our lives. This workbook includes so many effective strategies to help those of us who struggle because of perfectionism, and I plan to use it in my individual work with clients as well as with groups. I highly recommend this book to clinicians and the general public alike."

—**Laura Reagan, LCSW-C**, integrative trauma therapist, and host of
the *Therapy Chat* podcast

The CBT Workbook for Perfectionism

Evidence-Based Skills *to*
Help You Let Go *of* Self-Criticism,
Build Self-Esteem & Find Balance

SHARON MARTIN, MSW, LCSW

New Harbinger Publications, Inc.

Publisher's Note

NEW HARBINGER PUBLICATIONS is a registered trademark of New Harbinger Publications, Inc.

Copyright © 2019 by Sharon Martin
New Harbinger Publications, Inc.
5720 Shattuck Avenue
Oakland, CA 94609
www.ncwharbinger.com

Cover design by Amy Shoup

Acquired by Ryan Buresh

Edited by Jennifer Eastman

Library of Congress Cataloging-in-Publication Data

Names: Martin, Sharon C., 1971- author.
Title: The CBT workbook for perfectionism : evidence-based skills to help you let go of self-criticism, build self-esteem, and find balance / Sharon Martin ; foreword by Julie de Azevedo Hanks.
Description: Oakland, CA : New Harbinger Publications, 2019. | Includes bibliographical references.
Identifiers: LCCN 2018031431 (print) | LCCN 2018033637 (ebook) | ISBN 9781684031542 (PDF e-book) | ISBN 9781684031559 (ePub) | ISBN 9781684031535 (paperback)
Subjects: LCSH: Perfectionism (Personality trait) | Anxiety. | Self-actualization (Psychology) | Self-esteem. | BISAC: SELF-HELP / Anxieties & Phobias. | SELF-HELP / Personal Growth / Self-Esteem.
Classification: LCC BF698.35.P47 (ebook) | LCC BF698.35.P47 M37 2019 (print) | DDC 155.2/32--dc23
LC record available at https://lccn.loc.gov/2018031431

Printed in the United States of America

26	25	24				
15	14	13	12	11	10	9

Contents

Foreword

In a culture obsessed with appearance and performance, it's all too easy to fall into the trap of perfectionism. I've personally fallen into this trap and have had to gain skills to overcome perfectionism, as have many of my clients during over two decades of clinical practice. Yet there are few resources that tackle perfectionism specifically, and none that are so actionable and practical as Sharon Martin's book *The CBT Workbook for Perfectionism*.

Because Sharon and I work with similar clientele—highly motivated and gifted individuals who find themselves feeling burdened, chronically unhappy, and emotionally drained—I was excited to see what new insights and resources she would bring to the process of overcoming perfectionism. I've been looking for this kind of workbook for years!

Perfectionism manifests in people who want to excel, who care about their families, and who work hard in their careers. As a licensed counselor, Sharon speaks with authority and wisdom, but not pretension, offering exercises to walk you though each process step-by-step. I found her work to be enlightening, as it makes use of both evidence-based strategies and real-life clinical examples from her own career as a clinician.

Drawing upon relevant psychological subtopics (such as Brené Brown's research on shame and Kristin Neff's writings about self-compassion), Sharon explores perfectionism in depth: where it stems from, what it looks like in action, how it negatively affects health and relationships, how it can keep us from taking risks or moving forward, and most importantly, how to utilize proven strategies to effectively manage it so that it doesn't control us.

From a stylistic standpoint, I am impressed by the structure of this workbook. Each chapter in the heart of the book serves as a bridge to move from a negative thought pattern or habit to a positive one (such as "From Busy to Mindfully Present" and "From Guilt to Self-Care"), which conveys optimism and confidence that the reader really can reach a place of peace. And as the name indicates, this is truly a workbook, complete with reflective questions and activities to help readers apply the principles they learn to their actual life experiences.

Throughout the clinical examples given in the book, Sharon highlights the trend that individuals struggling with perfectionism initially believe that lowering their expectations or cutting themselves slack in any way will be akin to failure. This echoes what I've seen in my own career and life: sometimes we push back against the idea of letting go of the ideal because we assume it means surrendering to being mediocre, but in reality, the opposite is true. This book as a whole helps illustrate how freeing ourselves from the stranglehold of perfectionism allows us to pursue *excellence*. And perhaps most importantly, letting go of perfectionism means that we're better able to authentically connect with other people in a meaningful way.

If you struggle with not feeling good enough, if you want to break out of unhealthy thinking errors and comparisons that hold you back, I highly recommend Sharon's one-of-a-kind workbook to teach you actionable steps to overcome the emotional plague of perfectionism and instead find freedom, fulfillment, and connection.

—Julie de Azevedo Hanks, PhD, LCSW
Author of *The Assertiveness Guide For Women* and *The Burnout Cure*
Owner and executive director of Wasatch Family Therapy

Acknowledgments

Bringing a book from idea to publication is quite an endeavor and certainly not something one does alone. So I want to express my gratitude to everyone who has supported this project. First, I'd like to thank New Harbinger Publications for the opportunity to write this book. In particular, I'm grateful to the editorial staff, especially Ryan Buresh for his guidance throughout the entire process and Erin Raber and Vicraj Gill for their feedback and support in organizing and improving my writing. And special thanks to my copy editor, Jennifer Eastman, for helping to put all the final details in place.

I also want to extend a huge thank you to Julie de Azevedo Hanks, PhD. In addition to generously writing the foreword to this book, Julie has been a mentor and role model. She's an example of a fellow social worker who's improving people's lives through her writing and work in the media—things I never saw myself doing but now find so gratifying. Julie encouraged me to dream bigger and take chances, giving me the final push to start writing my blog, *Happily Imperfect*, which eventually led to my writing this book.

Thank you to my family, friends, and colleagues for their interest in and support of my writing. I especially want to thank Michelle Farris for cheering me on every step of the way with her consistently positive can-do attitude and Mari Lee for the perfect balance of encouragement and accountability. And I'm grateful to my husband and children for their patience and giving me the time and space to write.

And, lastly, thank you to my clients who are truly my greatest teachers. Having the privilege of walking alongside them through life's darkest moments has been an inspiration and continuously reminds me of the power of the human spirit to overcome, grow, and change.

Introduction

Welcome to *The CBT Workbook for Perfectionism* and the next step in your journey to overcome perfectionism. Perhaps you picked up this book because you never seem to feel good enough—no matter how hard you try or how much you accomplish, it's never enough. Or perhaps you're physically and emotionally exhausted from trying to be everything to everyone. Or you procrastinate or fail to try things because you're afraid you won't be able to do them perfectly. Or maybe you're tired of beating yourself up over every mistake.

In the beginning, perfectionism often feels like a strength, a way to accomplish great things, be rewarded, and avoid criticism. But it also creates unnecessary stress and anxiety. It damages your self-esteem and can leave you feeling disconnected and unworthy. Eventually, perfectionism feels like more of a burden than an asset. If this has been your experience, and you're ready to tame your perfectionism and reclaim your life, this book can help!

The CBT Workbook for Perfectionism is about change, about keeping what works, modifying what doesn't, finding balance, creating meaningful relationships, and realizing that while hard work and achievements matter, they aren't always what matters most. My goal in writing this workbook is for you to find growth, not failure, in your mistakes and to be able to accept, not hate, your flaws. Overcoming perfectionism is a challenging process, but one that can bring greater joy and fulfillment to all areas of your life—family life, work and job satisfaction, friendships, and physical and mental health.

About This Book

This workbook is designed to help you understand the root causes of your perfectionism and provide you with practical tools for moderating your perfectionist tendencies. In chapters 1 and 2, you'll learn more about what constitutes perfectionism, how it causes problems in your daily life, and how to identify the particular ways that it shows up in your life. Chapter 3 explores how your childhood, especially how you were parented, led to the development of your perfectionist traits. In chapters 4 through 12, you'll target specific aspects of perfectionism—fear, self-criticism, procrastination, busyness, people-pleasing, anger, criticism of others, guilt, and shame—and work on exercises to help you change your perfectionist thoughts and actions in these areas. And chapter 13 concludes with strategies for staying motivated and maintaining the changes you've made.

I developed the exercises in this book over the course of twenty years as a psychotherapist and through my own efforts to overcome perfectionism. For me, learning how to change began with understanding the connection between my thoughts, feelings, and actions. It also included learning how to slow down, take better care of myself, and be kinder to myself. And as I shared these strategies with my clients, they found relief in them as well.

Many of the exercises in this book are based on the ideas of cognitive behavioral therapy (CBT), which explains how our thoughts influence our feelings and behaviors. You will learn how to intercept your rigid thoughts about success and failure; your exceptionally high expectations; your feelings of inadequacy, fear, and shame; and your perfectionist behaviors, such as procrastinating, overworking, and criticizing.

In addition to CBT, this book uses concepts of mindfulness and self-compassion. Mindfulness can help you tune in to the present, so you can thoughtfully make choices that reflect your true values and desires rather than overextending yourself due to people-pleasing and goal-oriented, achievement-driven pursuits intended to prove your worth. And self-compassion is a powerful way to combat self-criticism and learn to accept yourself just as you are.

How to Use This Workbook

The concepts and exercises in this book build upon each other, so it will make the most sense to start at the beginning and work your way through the book in the order in which it's laid out. Some chapters may speak more to your struggles than others, but most people will find some useful takeaways in every chapter. So I recommend trying all of the exercises at least once before deciding if they're helpful for you.

Practice

There isn't a quick fix for perfectionism; practice is key to making any type of lasting, meaningful change, and overcoming perfectionism is no different. Although some of the exercises in this book may result in immediate change or relief, many will need to be repeated multiple times to bring about the results you're looking for. For this reason, additional copies of some of the exercises can be printed from http://www.newharbinger.com/41535, so you can easily repeat them.

Allow Imperfection

Especially in the beginning, you may have a strong desire to answer the questions "correctly" or do the exercises perfectly, or feel pressure to understand all the concepts immediately. This isn't necessary. There are no grades or judgments. Instead, this is your opportunity to embrace your imperfections and learn to recognize them as a natural part of the human experience, not as shortcomings. The exercises should be challenging; this is how you grow and change. So try to allow yourself to do them imperfectly and learn by making mistakes. There's also no rush to finish this book. In fact, a slower pace can be quite useful, as it allows the ideas you learn to marinate and gradually become incorporated into your thoughts and actions.

Working with a Therapist

You can complete this workbook on your own or as an extension of your work with a therapist. Difficult feelings may come up as you work through this book. This is normal, and bringing emotions to the surface, so you can address them, can be an important part of the change process. However, if you experience increased symptoms of depression, anxiety, suicidal ideation, or an eating disorder, or if you feel overwhelmed, please consult with a mental health or medical professional immediately. A therapist can offer support and help tailor the exercises to your needs and assist you with other interventions, if needed.

Chapter 1

What Is Perfectionism?

Perfectionism can be confusing; it affects different people in different ways. But what we all have in common is that perfectionism can get in the way of living our lives to the fullest. It is the quest to be perfect or without flaws. It means we set impossibly high standards for ourselves and sometimes for others, and we believe that we should achieve our goals effortlessly and never make mistakes, have flaws, or be disagreeable. We consider anything less than perfect unacceptable and feel distressed when people (ourselves and others) don't live up to our expectations. But because our standards are unrealistic and unattainable, even with hard work, perfectionism is a losing proposition. It ultimately makes us feel worse rather than better.

In this chapter, we'll be looking at some of the most important aspects of perfectionism in order to understand it better, and we'll look at the different ways perfectionism shows up in people's lives.

Understanding Perfectionism

Perfectionism—the drive to achieve more, be more, and prove ourselves—can be so compelling that we feel driven to go, go, go. We can't stop. Loosening up or not pursuing perfection doesn't feel like an option, even when it's costing us dearly. This is the case for Laurie and

Jeremy. As you'll see in their stories that follow, their lives are different, but they share a relentless pursuit of perfection.

Laurie's Story

Laurie's a middle-aged mother of three. She jokingly says she should have been a firefighter, because she's always putting out fires. Laurie's tightly wound and competitive, and she demands a lot of herself and everyone around her—a true type A personality. She always seems to have a million things to do and lives with her phone implanted in one hand and her day planner in the other. Laurie's plagued with insomnia and feels like she can't "turn off her mind." Even when she's awake, she can't seem to relax. Her husband just wants her to sit through an entire movie with him without getting up to wash the last of the dishes or check her e-mail. Laurie never seems to do just one thing at a time. In fact, the only time Laurie slows down is when she's got an excruciating migraine, which seems to be happening more and more as she adds more commitments to her to-do list.

Jeremy's Story

Jeremy, thirty years old, is a doctor at a prestigious teaching hospital. By outward appearances, he's successful, but he feels miserable. His parents pushed him toward a career in medicine, while he had dreams of becoming a musician. Jeremy had played trumpet in the high school jazz band, and he'd excelled, as he did at everything he did. He was an excellent student, but that didn't seem to impress his parents. Their response to anything less than an A+ was to hang their heads in shame and quietly say, "You're not going to get into Stanford with these grades!" Never mind that Jeremy didn't want to go to Stanford or Harvard or any of the other universities his parents deemed worthy. His parents' criticism and high expectations ultimately did push Jeremy to study harder, go to Stanford, and become a doctor. He continues to push himself with late nights spent reviewing charts and taking additional training courses. He berates himself over the tiniest mistakes and has earned the nickname "Dr. Perfect" among the nurses, due to his demanding and critical treatment of them. But, truth be told, Jeremy feels anything but perfect.

You may notice similarities between your perfectionist traits and Laurie's or Jeremy's, but perfectionism can take many forms. We're going to take a closer look at some of the core features of perfectionism, and then you'll have an opportunity to think about what perfectionism looks like for you.

Painfully High Standards

High standards are a good thing; they encourage us to pursue excellence, solve problems, do quality work, create, and innovate. But high standards aren't the same as perfectionism or unrealistically high standards. Perfectionists strive to never make mistakes and are excruciatingly hard on themselves when they do.

People often confuse perfection with excellence. The pursuit of excellence is a healthy striving to be outstanding or above average. It promotes personal growth and improvement. But perfectionists don't expect just excellence; they have such painfully high standards that anything short of perfect is intolerable. Unlike seeking excellence, perfectionism is a narrow, intolerant expectation that we will never make mistakes or have any imperfections. The quest for excellence, on the other hand, allows for imperfections and mistakes; it's more forgiving than perfectionism.

The primary difference between pursuing excellence and perfection is the way making mistakes or having flaws is viewed. As perfectionists, we tend to overgeneralize mistakes and shortcomings. We take one mistake and use it to deem ourselves complete failures or inferior. This thinking error keeps perfectionists stuck on the negatives and unable to see the potentially positive aspects of mistakes and imperfections when in reality there are many benefits to embracing our imperfections and learning from our missteps.

When we expect perfection, we'll inevitably be disappointed. We all make mistakes, no matter how smart we are or how hard we work. Instead, we should strive for excellence. We can expect 100 percent from ourselves and others, but it's important to remember that 100 percent isn't perfection; it's the best that we can do at this moment, given these circumstances. Five years from now, I will probably be able to write an even better book than this one, because I'll continue to learn and develop new skills between now and then. That doesn't mean this is an inferior book; it's not perfect, but it's the best book I can write today, and that's all I can fairly ask of myself. Excellence is striving high, but offering yourself grace for mistakes made and things you don't yet know.

The Belief That Achievement Determines Self-Worth

Underneath our striving for perfection, there is likely a sense of inadequacy and insecurity. According to perfectionism researchers P. L. Hewitt, G. L. Flett, and S. F. Mikail, "The central focus of most perfectionists is on the needs to perfect the self and to correct or hide aspects of themselves that they see as imperfect" (2017, 23–24). They describe these strivings as an attempt to overcompensate for our perceived imperfections, and this makes it impossible for us to enjoy our successes and accomplishments. Perfectionism is an attempt to prove that we are secure, adequate, and in control.

As perfectionists, we base our self-worth on our performance and achievements. We aren't particularly resilient, in that we don't easily bounce back from setbacks; mistakes stick with us, damage our self-esteem, and leave us feeling worthless or incompetent. The only way we feel valued or worthy is by achieving, winning, and being flawless. This means that when we mess up or fail to achieve a goal, we see these mistakes as monumental. Other people might shrug off being late to an appointment as no big deal, but perfectionists see this as a personal failing resulting in damage to their self-esteem. Likewise, we aren't happy with a second-place finish. For some people, a silver medal would be a source of pride, but for us, it's a reminder that we still aren't the best or living up to our potential.

Perfectionists tend to be driven, high achievers. We're excellent at setting goals, and we often achieve them; this is how we measure our value as people. Perfectionists think, "I have to constantly work harder, contribute more, and only when I'm without criticism or flaws will I matter and have earned the right to be here." This puts intense pressure on us, because if we stop producing and perfecting, we feel worthless. There is no middle ground for perfectionists.

Perfectionists also let others determine their self-worth. We believe that self-worth must be earned, and we're only successful if others approve of us and our accomplishments. In this way, we allow others to determine our self-worth.

Fear

As we dig beneath the surface of all these efforts to prove ourselves worthy, we find fear and anxiety; there's a deep need to be liked, accepted, and valued. Perfectionists are afraid to disappoint or displease others (as I mentioned earlier, this shows up as people-pleasing behaviors and playing it safe) and don't want to reveal their struggles, weaknesses, and vulnerabilities, for fear of judgment. As perfectionists, we fear failure because we see failure as catastrophic and permanent. We'll do anything to avoid failure because we don't define failure as an event; we believe it's our identity. Failure is proof that we're inadequate, and perfectionism is a constant and intense need to *not* be inadequate—or even average.

Perfectionists try to avoid failure, criticism, and embarrassment by sticking to things they're already good at. We avoid risk and the unknown in favor of consistency, what's already known, and what feels safe.

How do you define perfectionism? Write your own personal definition of perfectionism.

_____

_____

_____

_____

How Perfectionism Manifests in Your Life

Perfectionism can be obvious or it can be quite subtle. Sometimes it's hard to spot, because it doesn't impact all areas of your life. It's possible for perfectionism to be causing problems in some areas of your life, but not others.

One helpful way of understanding perfectionism is the three personality traits identified by P. L. Hewitt and G. L. Flett (1991):

- **Self-oriented perfectionism:** This is a self-imposed expectation that you will be perfect. You create unrealistically high standards for yourself, that are not attainable. You are goal oriented and driven. In response to unrealistically high standards, you are highly self-critical. You notice every flaw and mistake, ruminate about them, and beat yourself up over them.

- **Other-oriented perfectionism:** You have unrealistic expectations of others. You expect perfection from others, and when they fail to live up to that, you are critical and easily find fault or assign blame. You're highly critical of others and frequently feel disappointed and angry that others aren't living up to your expectations.

- **Socially prescribed perfectionism:** You believe that others have abnormally high expectations of you that are impossible to meet.

In my clinical work, I notice that perfectionism involves a combination of impossibly high standards and high levels of criticism. And both high standards and criticism can be directed toward yourself or toward others (or both). People often have a combination of the three perfectionist personality traits. For example, earlier in the chapter, I told you about Jeremy, who had all three traits: He demanded perfection from himself, worked too much, and was self-critical. He criticized the nurses and gave no allowances for their mistakes. And his parents imposed unrealistically high expectations.

Perfectionism can impact any or all of these areas:

- **Professional accomplishments:** You work nonstop and expect professional achievements like earning promotions, winning the biggest accounts, being the top salesperson, and having financial success.

- **Parenting:** You expect that you and your spouse or partner will be perfect parents, and you demand perfection from your children. You want it to seem like parenting is always fun and easy and like your children are successful in all they do.

- **Body, weight, or physical appearance:** You're highly critical of and preoccupied with what you look like and being judged based on your appearance, and you never feel thin enough, tall enough, toned enough, or attractive enough.

- **Academic performance:** When in school, you expected to get more than a 4.0 GPA and be valedictorian, and you believed your future success rested on your academic performance.

- **Athletic abilities or fitness:** Sports and fitness aren't things you pursue for fun or simply to stay in shape. You're a driven athlete, expecting yourself to excel in all athletic pursuits. You compete competitively, constantly raising the bar, and pushing yourself beyond the limits of most people of similar age or fitness level.

- **Physical environment:** You expect your home and office to be neat, clean, and orderly. You might consider yourself a neat freak and feel anxious and overwhelmed when things are disorganized, not in their proper place, or messy. Your need for order and cleanliness can be so compelling that you have to clean and straighten your physical environment before you can relax, engage in meaningful conversation, or attend to other tasks.

- **The "perfect" life:** You need your life, family, and self to appear perfect and shiny on the outside—so everyone can see how wonderful it is. You want your home to look like it belongs on the cover of a home decor magazine, your children to behave impeccably, your clothes to be of the newest designer labels, and your marriage or relationship to be a picture-perfect romance with your soul mate.

Where do you notice perfectionism in your life?

_____

_____

_____

_____

_____

Perfectionist Thinking

Perfectionism shows up in our thinking as well as our behavior. Throughout this book, I'll share more about the connection between your thoughts, feelings, and actions and, in particular, how changing your thoughts can lead to behavior change. For now, let's begin to get a sense of what perfectionist thinking sounds like.

Perfectionists tend to see things as black or white; they define themselves and their actions as absolutes. "If I don't succeed at this, I'm a failure"—there's no middle ground to a perfectionist. Clearly, no one wants to be whatever negative label you're assigning to yourself (failure, loser, fat, stupid, lazy), so the only alternative, according to this way of thinking, is to impose more pressure and higher demands and become intolerant of mistakes, imperfections, or anything that keeps you from being the top performer.

Perfectionists believe that if they don't strive for perfection, they'll end up being mediocre. And mediocrity really means *inferiority* to a perfectionist.

Perfectionists overemphasize their weaknesses and underestimate their strengths. We have an easier time noticing mistakes or flaws and a harder time noticing our strengths. For example, you might discount the ten things you completed on your to-do list and only focus on and berate yourself for the one thing left undone. Or you might do the same to your spouse when you come home and immediately notice the dishes in the sink and kids' jackets strewn across the floor but fail to notice that your wife fed the kids, gave them baths, and has them tucked into bed. You're filtering out the positives.

Perfectionist thinking is based on a belief that we're inadequate: "I'm not enough, and the only way to be enough is to accomplish _____." This way of thinking means we always have to work to prove ourselves. We can never stop working, because as soon as we accomplish today's goal, we'll set a new one, and on and on. Perfectionist thinking sets us up to spend our days on the perfectionism hamster wheel. We're always chasing our self-worth, but we'll never find it as a perfectionist, because being perfect is an impossibility.

Jot down a few examples of your perfectionist thinking.

_____

_____

_____

_____

_____

Summary

As you know, perfectionism can be a stressful experience. It's riddled with painfully high standards, the false belief that achievement determines our self-worth, and fear. Now that we've identified some of the most common aspects of perfectionism and how it manifests in our actions and thinking, we're ready to delve deeper into understanding and changing your particular perfectionist behaviors. In chapter 2, you'll identify the specific ways that perfectionism shows up in your life. This will help you target your change efforts to address the areas where perfectionism is causing you the most problems.

Chapter 2

What Perfectionism Looks Like in Your Life

In chapter 1, we took a look at what perfectionism looks like in general. Now, we'll turn our attention to what perfectionism looks like for you specifically and how it may be negatively impacting your life. Having a clear understanding of your perfectionist traits and the resulting problems will help you focus your change efforts on your particular areas of struggle. And lastly, we'll explore the benefits of perfectionism, so you can moderate, rather than completely discard, those aspects of your perfectionism that serve you well.

Identifying Your Perfectionist Traits

Perfectionism looks a little different for everyone. Some of your perfectionist traits may be obvious to you, but you may uncover some other perfectionist traits that are more subtle or hidden through the checklist and questions in this chapter.

The perfectionist traits checklist that follows isn't a test that will be scored. It's not designed to tell you definitively whether you're a perfectionist or not. Perfectionism isn't an all-or-nothing characteristic; there isn't a threshold that says if you have X number of these traits, you're officially a perfectionist. In fact, it doesn't actually matter how many of the traits you check off.

My aim is to provide you with insights into yourself, so you can work on changing the particular perfectionist behaviors and thought patterns that get in the way of you living a fulfilling life.

Which of these traits describe you?

☐ You set exceptionally high standards for yourself.

☐ You have high standards for others and find they often don't live up to them.

☐ You feel others have unrealistic expectations of you.

☐ You're concerned about errors or mistakes.

☐ You're goal driven.

☐ You never feel satisfied; there's always more to do or accomplish.

☐ You're sensitive to criticism and try to avoid it.

☐ You're detail oriented.

☐ You're highly self-critical.

☐ You're critical of others.

☐ You're afraid of disappointing people.

☐ Your expectations are often unrealistic, leading to disappointment or frustration.

☐ You're always busy.

☐ You rarely take a sick day.

☐ You crave organization, lists, planners, charts, and data.

☐ You try to avoid making mistakes, and you see them as bad.

☐ You dwell on your mistakes and imperfections.

☐ You base your worth as a person on your accomplishments.

☐ Even when you succeed, you feel like it's not enough or that you could have done better.

☐ You'd rather do things yourself than have someone else do them "wrong."

☐ Sometimes it takes you a long time to finish things, because you redo, check, and try to make them perfect.

☐ You worry a lot about what people think of you.

☐ You try to avoid conflicts.

☐ You procrastinate or don't start things, because you don't think you can do them perfectly.

☐ People have judged you harshly in the past.

☐ You're afraid to fail.

☐ You feel angry or resentful.

☐ You feel defective or flawed.

☐ A change of plans can be upsetting to you.

☐ You ruminate or overthink things.

☐ You have stress-related health problems such as headaches, gastrointestinal problems, or high blood pressure.

☐ You play it safe.

☐ You don't like to try new things, especially when there's a chance of embarrassment, incompetence, or not being as good as everyone else.

☐ You're a workaholic, putting in long hours and missing out on leisure activities because you have to work.

☐ You have a hard time relaxing.

☐ You have insomnia or trouble sleeping.

☐ You have trouble being happy for others' success.

☐ You don't like to share your weaknesses or vulnerabilities with others.

☐ You tend to feel tense, stressed, or anxious.

☐ You need to win at all costs.

☐ You think that if you were really smart or talented, you wouldn't have to work so hard.

☐ You demand a lot of others.

☐ You're frequently disappointed when people fail to meet your expectations.

☐ You have difficulty being spontaneous.

☐ You believe that a single failure or flaw defines you.

☐ You want to feel in control at all times.

☐ Despite many signs of success, you don't actually feel successful.

Which perfectionist traits cause you the most distress? Identify the three to five most problematic traits you have, and describe how often you experience them.

_____

_____

_____

_____

_____

_____

_____

_____

How Does Your Perfectionism Impact Your Life?

Let's take a look at how your perfectionist traits are impacting your life in order to get a clearer picture of how your life can improve by being more compassionate and realistic.

Stress

I have never met a perfectionist who wasn't stressed! When things are going well—you're achieving your goals, and life is generally going as planned—perfectionism may not cause you many obvious problems. But if it's your nature to demand a lot from yourself, work harder than most, and sacrifice sleep and rest to fulfill one more obligation or do one more thing, you're going to feel stressed, due to the pressure you put on yourself both emotionally and physically.

Stress can show up in our bodies as aches and pains, insomnia and trouble sleeping, gastrointestinal problems, muscles tension, and low energy. Stress also impacts our mood, contributing to anxiety, depression, and a short temper. Some perfectionists have trouble managing their emotions when they get angry, disappointed, or frustrated, and others shut themselves off from their feelings. You may blow up over seemingly small problems or changes. Or you may go the opposite route, becoming quite unemotional, because you're trying to cope by ignoring, distracting, or numbing yourself to avoid feeling the things that stress you out. Neither is an effective way to deal with your feelings. A build-up of negative feelings (anger, hurt, disappointment, frustration, fear, sadness) contributes not only to stress and tension but also to larger problems like anxiety and depression.

Perfectionists also tend to struggle even more than the average person when life takes an unexpected turn, whether it's moving, the death of a loved one, the stock market plummeting, or failing to meet a goal. We often have a hard time recovering from setbacks such as these, because we're apt to focus on the negatives, let single events define us, and think in rigid, all-or-nothing parameters. These things make it tough for us to roll with the punches and adjust when life feels out of control or just isn't going the way we'd hoped or expected. As a result, we seem to overreact when we experience disappointments, failures, or unplanned events.

Even though I've come a long way with my own perfectionism, I still find it challenging to quiet my mind. I tend to have so many ideas and worries that my brain is in overdrive. (Later in the book, I'll share with you some of the techniques I use to stop worrying and relax.) This is common among perfectionists and overachievers—we have busy minds, which is not surprising, given all the balls we're juggling. And we tend to overthink things, as well as to ruminate or think about the same things over and over again, which not only interferes with productivity but also increases our stress level. For me, this shows up as difficulty making decisions. When we believe it's imperative that we choose the perfect color to paint the house or the perfect outfit to wear to an important meeting, it gets overwhelming and analysis paralysis can set in. We agonize about needing to get it right, as if there is only one nice color to paint the house or wearing the wrong suit will have dire consequences.

How does the stress of perfectionism negatively impact your health? Do you have physical symptoms, like trouble sleeping, headaches, backaches, or gastrointestinal issues? Does stress exacerbate a chronic illness or medical condition?

_____

_____

_____

_____

What about mental health concerns like feelings of depression, anxiety, or anger? Do you think stress contributes to those?

_____

_____

_____

_____

When you encounter setbacks, how do you typically feel? And how do you respond?

_____

_____

_____

_____

Do you experience overthinking or difficulty making decisions?

_____

_____

_____

_____

Work-Life Balance

Working eighty hours a week is exhausting, no matter whether it's at an office, as a volunteer, or as a caregiver and household manager for your family. One of the natural consequences of working so much is that we don't have time or energy for other things, such as hobbies, relationships, fun and play, vacations, or daily rest and relaxation. We simply can't do everything, and as perfectionists, we often choose work or put other people's needs above our own. You may be thinking, *Work is important, and I put in all those hours because I have to.* Sometimes working long hours is necessary, but perfectionists tend to work excessively, either out of duty and not wanting to disappoint people or because they genuinely love to work and get great satisfaction from a job well done. In either case, there are often changes that we can make to bring our lives into better balance. Mei and Chris, both overworked teachers, illustrate how work and personal life can be out of balance when perfectionists feel driven to work excessively.

Mei's Story

Mei is an enthusiastic young fifth-grade teacher at an urban public school. She routinely gets to school at six thirty in the morning in order to do lesson planning and grading. She has an open-door policy, which means her students can stop by before school, during lunch, or after school for extra help. During most lunch periods, Mei has a group of girls come to eat lunch and chat with her. Between meetings, straightening up her classroom, and directing the school musical, it's unusual if she leaves school before six. Evenings and weekends are spent grading papers, making costumes, and learning creative new approaches to teach her students. Mei loves her job and her students. She sees teaching as her calling and feels it's essential that she's a positive role model and inspiration, as many of her students don't have anyone at home who encourages their academic and emotional growth. Mei gave up on dating, because she doesn't have time, and her friends have stopped calling, because she always turns down their invitations to happy hour or weekend barbeques. At this point, her social life consists of dinner with her parents on Sunday nights.

Chris's Story

Of course, not everyone who spends a lot of time at work enjoys it. Chris is a committed high school math teacher who also puts in long hours. Unlike Mei, he resents having to spend his evenings and weekends working. He'd rather be spending time with his wife and kids or restoring classic cars with his brother. Everything about his job seems to irritate Chris—he can't take a real lunch break, the students are disruptive and unmotivated, and the parents expect an immediate response to their frequent e-mails. Chris had to give up his morning run when he got roped into coaching swimming before school four days a week. However, Chris made a commitment to teaching for two more years, and he'll see it through despite feeling resentful and burned-out.

Perfectionists are workhorses, and despite our fatigue and overwhelm, people count on us to get things done—and we generally come through for them. You may work nonstop because you love it, like Mei, or out of obligation or fear, like Chris, but the end result is always that our personal life, our hobbies, and our fun and self-care fall by the wayside.

Another challenge that perfectionists often have with hobbies and recreation is that we turn them into competitions and situations where we feel compelled to excel and prove our worth. So we might take a casual weekend soccer game and turn it into a competition; we get fixated on winning, playing by the rules, or micromanaging the game. Or we take a painting class with a friend, and instead of going with the flow, we want our painting to be exactly like the example. This can suck the fun right out of activities that are meant to be low-key opportunities to kick back, relax, and bond with our friends and family.

What would happen if you worked less?

_____

_____

_____

_____

_____

What drives you to work so much?

_____

_____

_____

_____

_____

What are you giving up in order to work so much?

_____

_____

_____

_____

_____

_____

What do you do for fun? What do you do to relax? Do you prioritize time for hobbies or relaxation?

_____

_____

_____

_____

_____

_____

Can you keep a hobby light and fun, or does it turn into a competitive or perfectionist endeavor?

_____

_____

_____

_____

_____

Are there things that you used to do for fun, but now you've quit, because you don't have time or it doesn't seem important?

_____

_____

_____

_____

Missed Opportunities

In addition to our busyness, we miss out on a lot of life's pleasures because of fear. Our fears can be so deep that we actually convince ourselves that we don't want to do things rather than tap into the awareness that we're afraid of failure, embarrassment, criticism, rejection, and not being as good as everyone else. These fears can prevent us from doing specific things, like public speaking or joining a community softball league. And despite being high achievers, our fears hold us back from doing things that might enhance our lives. These could be business opportunities, forming new relationships, traveling, or hobbies. We like to stick to things we know we're good at; this way, we're assured success and accolades (or at least not embarrassment and criticism). Because our self-worth hinges on our performance, we work really hard at avoiding things that are new and different.

Think about things you're not doing because you might not be good at them. Do you avoid joining the softball team because you might look foolish? Have you given up on dating because you're tired of the rejection? Do you avoid parties and get-togethers because they're a waste of time?

How do you play it safe in your life? Are there opportunities that you've passed up or things you've quit or haven't even bothered trying because you might not be good at them?

_____

_____

_____

_____

The flip side is that we may also continue to do unsatisfying things for the same reasons—fear of failure, embarrassment, criticism, rejection, and not being as good as everyone else. Chris, the high school teacher, is a good example of this. He's clearly unhappy in his job, but he stays, because it's what he's always done and he knows he's good at it. Starting over with a new job or career feels daunting. Sometimes we choose the devil we know over the uncertainty of making a change. In these circumstances, our perfectionism and pursuit of achievement above all else can keep us from pursuing new opportunities that could lead to growth, creativity, greater success, and satisfaction.

Are there things that you continue to do or relationships you maintain because you're afraid a change will be worse than what you're doing now?

_____

_____

_____

_____

_____

_____

_____

Relationships

Relationships are another area where we pay a steep price for our perfectionism. First, we generally don't prioritize our relationships. We're all about work first and play later. And let's be honest, the work never ends, so we don't play! Fear and busyness cause us to put relationships, like hobbies, into the "unnecessary" category. But this leaves us unsatisfied and questioning what's wrong with us.

Being connected to and accepted by others is a universal human desire. Humans were designed to depend on each other and live in community. But over the years, across Western culture, and particularly in America, we've promoted work, individual achievement, and independence over interdependence, cooperation, and balanced living. Our fierce independence has translated into permission to work ourselves to death, pushing people away and insisting that we can do it all ourselves.

Understandably, it sometimes feels easier to do everything ourselves. When we rely on others, we can be let down and frustrated, but focusing on achievement over relationships can be a lonely and painful experience. We all want to feel understood, loved, and needed. We want to care for others and be cared for. We want to belong. Perfectionism can be a barrier to connection by making us feel separate, different, and less than.

Relationships require our emotional and physical presence. Our relationships will suffer if we're putting the bulk of our time and energy into working, training, or pursuing our next goal. We can get so busy or goal driven that we don't prioritize quality time with our friends or family. Some perfectionists are physically present in their relationships, but mentally distracted. Your mind may be caught up in ruminating about the past or worrying about the future. Or you may just be juggling so many things that you're perpetually distracted. It's entirely possible to be in the same physical space but not be connected to others. In chapter 1, I told you about Laurie, whose husband just wanted her to sit down and watch an entire movie with him. He wanted to connect with her, put his head on her lap, and laugh at the same jokes with her. Instead, she would take out her laptop and multitask or get up to wash some dishes. Her husband felt rejected and taken for granted. It didn't seem like Laurie really cared about spending time with him.

Have you neglected your relationships? Do you spend quality time with your partner or family? Have you lost touch with friends because you're too busy?

_____

_____

_____

_____

_____

_____

In addition to quality time, relationships also require vulnerability. You may be married and have plenty of friends but wonder if you feel truly connected to them. In these cases, perfectionism can act as a shield that we use to keep people—our coworkers, our family, our friends, even our spouse and children—at a distance, allowing them to see only the parts of us that we feel are perfect or pleasing. But relationships without depth and vulnerability can feel shallow and leave us questioning whether we're truly loved and accepted. Deep inside, we may still be afraid that if we show our messy, imperfect selves, we won't be loved. That fear of not being good enough convinces us to keep the imperfect pieces of ourselves hidden.

Do your friends and family know the real you? Do you share your secrets and intimate thoughts and dreams, or do you tend keep relationships superficial? Do you confide in others about your struggles, worries, and failures?

_____

_____

_____

_____

_____

_____

Do you worry about what your friends and family would think if they knew your inner thoughts or missteps?

_____

_____

_____

_____

_____

_____

If perfectionism has been a barrier to deep connection with others, how have your relationships suffered as a result?

_____

_____

_____

_____

_____

_____

_____

_____

_____

_____

_____

Perfectionists can also be quite critical of others. If we demand perfection from our spouse, kids, or coworkers, we're probably frequently frustrated with them, and this frustration often comes out as criticism. Frequent and harsh criticism hurts relationships. It doesn't feel good to be criticized. People will naturally pull away from someone who is always pointing out their flaws and telling them they're doing things wrong. People may tiptoe around, afraid to upset us, feeling like they can't be themselves around us because of our intolerance for imperfection. Our friends and family may be outwardly angry with us for the way we criticize them. Or, more likely, they put up with our perfectionist criticism but are secretly resentful of it. Our critical and controlling behaviors may or may not be effective at getting others to behave as we feel they should, but odds are, they're damaging our relationships.

How have your relationships been negatively affected by your critical and controlling behaviors? If you're not sure, consider telling your close friends and family that you are working on changing and that it would be helpful to understand how your criticism impacts them. Or try to put yourself in their shoes and think about how it might feel to be criticized regularly.

_____

_____

_____

_____

_____

_____

Might your relationships be better if you could be more accepting of other people's imperfections? How?

_____

_____

_____

_____

_____

_____

_____

What Perfectionist Traits Do You Most Want to Change?

As we move through this book, we'll take an even deeper look at the major ways that perfectionism costs us physical health, relationships, fun, opportunities, creativity, peace of mind, deep connection with others, and self-acceptance. And we'll learn ways we can change these patterns.

Before we move on, try to identify a few of the changes you most want to make.

What do you do as a perfectionist that you'd like to stop doing?

_____

_____

_____

_____

_____

What does perfectionism prevent you from doing? Is there an opportunity you'd pursue or a risk you would take if perfectionism weren't standing in your way?

_____

_____

_____

_____

_____

Which of your relationships do you most want to change or repair?

_____

_____

_____

_____

_____

Does Your Perfectionism Have Any Benefits?

To be fair, perfectionism isn't all bad. I want to assure you that the goal of this book isn't for you to throw out all of the traits that have contributed to your success and accomplishments. Many of them are beneficial, and with modification, they can be important pieces of creating the life you want.

However, as we've noted, perfection isn't achievable, and in trying to pursue it, we often create a great deal of suffering for ourselves and others. But with some tweaks, we can be successful and fulfilled. It's important that we distinguish unhealthy perfectionism from healthy striving for excellence and hard work. So, let's consider which aspects of your perfectionism are worth keeping and how we can adjust them to work better for you.

How is perfectionism helpful or beneficial to you?

_____

_____

_____

_____

_____

Which perfectionist traits are you reluctant to give up?

_____

_____

_____

_____

_____

_____

What concerns you about giving up perfectionism? Do you think you can still achieve your goals without perfectionism?

_____

_____

_____

_____

_____

_____

_____

_____

_____

_____

How do you think your life might be better if you could tame your perfectionism?

_____

_____

_____

_____

_____

_____

_____

Summary

Many of you have been willing to pay the steep price that comes with perfectionism, but you picked up this book because perfectionism also causes some problems in your life. Now that you've got a clearer picture of how perfectionism can contribute to stress, overworking, missed opportunities, and feeling disconnected and lonely, you're probably able to see how modifying some of your perfectionist traits can bring more contentment to your life. Moving forward, we're going to look at where these perfectionist traits came from. Gaining a greater understanding of the roots of our perfectionism can help us to be both more self-compassionate and more adept at changing them.

Chapter 3

Uncovering the Roots of Your Perfectionism

It's normal to want to understand where your perfectionist traits originated. People are complex, and there isn't one single cause of perfectionism. Your present self is a complicated and synergistic combination of your biology and experiences. As we explore the roots of perfectionism, we'll specifically look at how your childhood experiences, including your gender, culture, and the way you were parented, impacted your beliefs about yourself and the expectations you have for yourself.

Many perfectionists grew up with unrealistic expectations from parents or caretakers, or even themselves. Often, perfectionism is encouraged in families, communities, and institutions. Sometimes parents require straight As in school and flawless piano recitals; they knowingly or unknowingly establish perfection as the standard. For other children, perfectionism is self-imposed. Your parents may not have expected perfection, but you set this standard for yourself as a result of the culture and community expectations that surrounded you.

When no one explicitly accepts you just as you are—when you always feel you must earn or prove your worth—you turn to achievement as a measure of self-worth. I want to help you untangle this connection. Your achievements are not who you are. Success is not a measure of your worth. You are so much more than your resume or a shelf full of trophies.

Childhood Experiences

We all hold certain beliefs about ourselves. You might see yourself as hardworking or overly sensitive or capable or not creative. You're probably aware of some of these beliefs, but many are in our subconscious and influence our thinking and actions without us realizing they're even there.

Your parents or primary caregivers were the single biggest influences on how you came to see yourself. Young children believe what their parents tell them. If an adult tells a small child that he or she is a failure, not smart enough, too fat, or not talented, the child will accept this as fact and internalize these beliefs about himself or herself. The child then continues to unconsciously find evidence to support this belief. So, if your mother has been telling you that you're fat since you were four years old, you probably still think you're unattractive or overweight, or you worry about your weight (unless you've worked hard to undo this belief). This was the case for Kayla. These early messages from her mother became ingrained, because she unconsciously reinforced them by repeating them to herself and assuming that others thought the same. For example, she misinterpreted her dear friend's aloof response to her new outfit as critical when, in reality, her friend was just preoccupied with something else.

To understand where your perfectionist self-story originated, try to recall some of the early messages you received about who you are and what makes you worthy or unworthy.

What messages did your parents or caregivers give you? What did they say or do repeatedly that formed the roots of your identity and self-esteem?

_____

_____

_____

_____

_____

_____

_____

As we grow up, our brains develop, and we gain the thinking skills and life experience to understand that sometimes adults are wrong. But children are at the mercy of adults when it comes to building their self-worth. Young children also naturally have a strong desire to please their parents or caregivers. It's a survival instinct, given that young children are unlikely to survive without a caregiver. It's also why children continue to try to please their parents even when they are abused or neglected or when their parents are constantly critical and demeaning. If you haven't already, try on the idea that your parents' appraisal of you isn't the be-all and end-all of who you are. Now that you're an adult, you can form your own self-assessment, which may be quite different than the early messages you got from your parents.

How does it feel to consider that your parents were misguided or wrong in their appraisal of you? Can you see that the labels they used to define you are not completely accurate?

_____

_____

_____

_____

_____

_____

_____

_____

Because our coping skills, personality traits, habits, and the way we see ourselves and the world can usually be traced back to childhood, we're going to take a look at four parenting styles that can lead to perfectionism. As you read, consider the extent to which your parents' parenting style fits each description.

Demanding Parents

Some parents demand perfection from their children. Demanding parents value achievements—external markers of success such as awards, grades, money, titles, and prestige—and are overly concerned with what other people think. They see their children as an extension of and reflection of themselves. Therefore, demanding parents actually derive some of their own self-esteem from their kids' achievements. They feel embarrassed or inadequate if their children are less than perfect.

Jeremy, the doctor that I told you about in chapter 1, had demanding parents. They were ashamed when he didn't get an A+ in a class, and they expected him to go to Stanford or Harvard and become a doctor, even though that wasn't what Jeremy wanted. They didn't seem to care that he dreamed of becoming a musician. In their eyes, music was not a real career; it was a hobby.

Demanding parents tend to tell their children (even adult children) what to do rather than inquire about what the child wants, needs, or feels. This way of parenting is a dictatorship. The children must live up to their parents' expectations or there will be severe consequences.

Demanding parents rely on emotional control strategies to establish that success is a must and that there is no room for failure, insolence, or disobedience. Emotional abuse (excessive yelling, cursing, and name-calling—"stupid," "good for nothing," "failure"), manipulation, and passive-aggressive strategies (the silent treatment, withholding affection, guilt trips) are often employed by demanding parents.

They may also use physical discipline and punishment (such as beatings, locking children out of the house, or forcing children to stand in the corner for lengthy periods of time) to force their children to live up to their standards. Demanding parents behave in these ways out of frustration and anger toward the child, but they also feel justified and believe that harsh consequences will motivate their children to succeed.

The most profound consequence of demanding parenting, however, is the damage that is done to the child's self-esteem. Children with demanding parents become extremely hard on themselves. In my experience, they often experience anxiety and depression related to the pressure to perform and achieve. They constantly feel like they aren't living up to their parents' (and their own) expectations, leaving them with a sense of shame, failure, and inadequacy. They may have a hard time identifying what they really want and need, because they've internalized their parents' goals and expectations. They have difficulty asserting themselves, so there is often resentment and anger under the surface. Children with demanding parents also learn that love is conditional. They learn that they are loveable only when they please others. Perfection becomes a way to gain acceptance, love, and praise.

Did your parents display any of the traits of demanding parents?

☐ They valued achievements and external markers of success.

☐ They were concerned about what others thought.

☐ They felt embarrassed or inadequate if their children were less than perfect.

☐ They set unrealistically high expectations.

☐ They told their children what to do with little concern for the child's interests, dreams, or abilities.

☐ They micromanaged their children's social lives, academics, sports, or extracurricular activities.

☐ They were intolerant of mistakes and saw them as failures.

☐ They were rigid, all-or-nothing thinkers.

☐ They used emotional abuse such as yelling, name-calling, the silent treatment, withholding love, or guilt trips to shame and control.

☐ They were highly critical.

☐ They had strict rules and harsh consequences.

☐ They were physically abusive.

☐ They offered praise only for achievements.

☐ They provided minimal affection (loving words, hugs, kisses).

Perfectionist Parents

Perfectionism can also be learned by children growing up with goal-oriented, driven, perfectionist parents who modeled or rewarded this way of thinking and acting. Perfectionism is encouraged when children are praised excessively for their achievements rather than their efforts or progress. The focus is on what the children accomplish rather than the process or who they are as people.

Marco's Story

Marco, now a young adult struggling with his perfectionism, recalls his freshman year of high school. He had set his sights on making the varsity football team. He trained and practiced all summer, regardless of the heat or the fact that most of his friends were hanging out at the pool. Marco's parents had always encouraged him to aim high; they were proud of his work ethic and dedication. They never had to remind him to study or do his chores. Marco's dad was a well-known, high-powered divorce attorney. He was up at five o'clock in the morning, seven days a week, headed to the gym and then to work, and often wasn't home until after nine at night. Marco's dad liked to make sure everyone knew he was successful by insisting on hand-tailored suits, a new car every year, and a beach house (which he was too busy to enjoy). Sadly, Marco's father died of a heart attack when he was only fifty years old. Marco's mom is a homemaker and volunteer extraordinaire. Her house looks like a page out of a luxury magazine, and even when she was raising three boys, it was always pristine. She also keeps herself impeccably dressed and manicured. Marco can't remember ever seeing his mom without her hair and makeup done.

Marco was never satisfied with his grades, even though they were excellent, or his performance on the football field. He thought if he could just make the varsity team, then he'd be happy. So when he didn't make it, he sunk into a depression that his friends and teachers couldn't understand. They saw his perfect life, successful parents, and excellent grades and didn't understand why he was so down.

Perfectionist parents like Marco's are generally loving and don't necessarily directly set unrealistic expectations for their children (although they may, if they're demanding as well). They model their value of a perfect family, house, and appearance through achieving at extremely high levels and attaining academic, career, or monetary success. Their children are likely to hear them speak critically about themselves and compare themselves to others.

Did your parents display any of the traits of perfectionist parents?

- ☐ They were goal-oriented, driven perfectionists.
- ☐ They encouraged high achievement, goals, and standards.
- ☐ They praised their children's achievements rather than their efforts or progress.
- ☐ They were disciplined and rigid.
- ☐ They demanded a lot of themselves.
- ☐ They measured themselves and their children in comparison to others.
- ☐ They valued outward signs of success such as material possessions, awards, titles, and physical appearance in themselves and their children.
- ☐ They felt unhappy or unsatisfied despite outward signs of success.
- ☐ They unintentionally modeled self-criticism.

Distracted Parents

Many parents are so distracted that they aren't attuned to what their children need. Usually, these parents mean well but are unaware of how their children feel, what they need, and how their own behavior affects their children. A distracted parent could be one who works eighty hours a week and isn't physically or emotionally available. She could also be a parent who spends most of her time in front of a screen or with her nose in a book. And some distracted parents are so busy that they're always going from one activity or commitment to the next. They never slow down long enough to really check in with their children. Distracted parents usually meet their children's physical needs but often neglect their emotional needs. Perfectionism is a way for children of distracted parents to either get noticed or help their parents out.

Jacqueline's Story

Jacqueline is her mother's only child. Her father, on the other hand, has five more children with his second wife, and long ago Jacqueline realized that she is not among her father's favorites. Growing up, she saw her dad occasionally, as he only lived ten miles away, but their visits were awkward, and they didn't seem to have much in common. Jacqueline lived with her mother, who was devoted to giving Jacqueline all the opportunities for success that she never had. She worked full-time as a bank teller, four nights a week waiting tables, and occasionally helped her sister cater parties on the weekend. This was the only way she could afford to send Jacqueline to private school and soccer camp. Jacqueline's mother couldn't always get to the spelling bees and soccer games, but she always gave her a big kiss on the forehead and said, "Jacqueline, I just couldn't be prouder of you. Someday, you're going to be someone important. I just know it!"

As a teenager, Jacqueline spent a lot of time alone, studying. She wanted to make her mom proud, and she knew getting a scholarship to college was the way to do it. However, Jacqueline's mother was too distracted and busy working to realize that Jacqueline passed up party invitations and dating in order to study. Nor did she notice that Jacqueline was binging and purging and that she agonized over what to wear every morning.

Jacqueline had two distracted parents, and she longed for more emotional connection with them. Jacqueline became obsessed with her grades and her appearance, because she knew this would please her parents, and unconsciously she thought she'd gain their approval and attention if she were perfect.

It's important to note that although Jacqueline's mother seemed to be focused on her daughter's well-being, Jacqueline experienced it as an interest in her future success, not in her as a person; her mother's love felt conditional in this regard. Distracted parents can be like Jacqueline's mother—well-meaning, but distant—or like her father, who was largely physically and emotionally absent. Distracted parents often lack the skills to be more emotionally present. Often, their own parents were emotionally distant, so this level of attunement seems normal to them. They may not outwardly demand perfection, but some such parents give the message that success is what makes you worthwhile, while others relay the message that the child isn't enough (smart enough, cute enough, talented enough) to garner their attention.

Did your parents display any of the traits of distracted parents?

- ☐ They were unaware of their children's feelings and needs.

- ☐ They were physically absent.

- ☐ They were physically present, but emotionally distant.

- ☐ They were uncomfortable talking about feelings.

- ☐ They were always busy.

- ☐ They believed that if their children were achieving or *seemed* happy, they must have been doing fine.

Overwhelmed Parents

Overwhelmed parents lack the skills to effectively cope with life's challenges and their children's needs. Some parents are chronically overwhelmed due to their own trauma, mental illness, addiction, or cognitive impairment. Overwhelmed parents might also be dealing with a crisis such as a very sick child or relative, marital or relationship problems, or grief. Chronic stressors such as unemployment, poverty, health problems, or living in a violent community can also exceed a parent's ability to cope.

When a family is in a constant state of crisis or overwhelm, it is particularly detrimental to the children. A crisis disrupts a family's equilibrium. This disruption may be due to a finite event, such as a parent being unemployed for six months, and after the crisis has passed, the family may regain its footing, especially if it was functioning well beforehand. Or the disruption may be ongoing, because there is a chronic stressor or series of stressors, such as unemployment compounded by depression and alcohol abuse, and the parent doesn't recover and never maintains stable employment again. Children are more likely to develop perfectionist traits to cope with an overwhelming and chaotic home life when their family is chronically stressed and overwhelmed.

Overwhelmed parents aren't just distracted and fatigued; they aren't able to provide a safe and nurturing environment for their children. In overwhelmed families, there is either a lack of consistent rules and structure, virtually no rules, or overly harsh or arbitrary rules. And overwhelmed parents either have unrealistic expectations for their children, such as expecting a five-year-old to prepare and clean up his or her own meals, or no expectations, as if they've already decided their child is a hopeless failure who will never succeed. Often overwhelmed parents cannot fulfill their adult responsibilities, so things like childcare, cooking and cleaning, and providing emotional support often fall on the older children.

Life in an overwhelmed family is unpredictable and can be emotionally or physically unsafe. Children often struggle to fully understand what's happening. Although even very young children can instinctively sense that something is wrong in their family—their parents are stressed or their environment is unsafe—they probably can't identify or understand the nature of these problems. It's very confusing for children to have this sense that things are off, but not have adults openly talk about what's happening and help them to understand it. So when no one is talking about Dad's depression or Mom's addiction, children will assume that they are causing the problems and that the family will be happy and healthy if they can be "better" children. Kids come up with distorted thoughts such as *If I got better grades, my dad wouldn't be so stressed out* or *If I were a perfect kid, my mom wouldn't drink so much.* In addition, some overwhelmed parents overtly blame their children for the family's problems, which compounds a child's false belief that they are the problem.

Trying to be perfect can be a defense against a chaotic, unpredictable, or unsafe home. Some children with overwhelmed parents use perfectionism to try to exact control over themselves and others in order to feel more safe and secure. For example, teenagers might edit an essay for hours or measure their breakfast cereal before eating it in order to create a sense of control and predictability that they aren't getting from their parents. Children develop perfectionist traits as a way to compensate for feelings of blame and a deep sense of being flawed and inadequate. As you'll see in Rebecca's story, they come to believe that if they can be perfect, they will please their parents, solve their family's problems, or bring respect to their family.

Rebecca's Story

Rebecca is the oldest of three children. Her dad was an alcoholic, and her mom desperately tried to pretend that everything was normal in their family. Rebecca recalls that her dad would get home from work at four in the afternoon and immediately start admonishing Rebecca and her siblings for making too much noise, for their grades, their appearance—pretty much anything he could think of. This continued until he was so drunk that he passed out on the couch. By dinnertime he was slurring his words, sometimes barely able to make it to the table without falling down. Rebecca's mother served dinner, made small talk, and ignored the fact that Dad was nearly incoherent. Rebecca tried to please her parents, but her father never acknowledged anything she did right, whether it was getting her driver's license or cleaning up all of his beer cans. When Rebecca made honor roll, her dad's response was, "Now, if only there was something you could do about that fat ass of yours!" Her mom was too busy dealing with her dad and her brother, who was frequently in trouble at school, to give Rebecca any positive attention. She counted on Rebecca to help with the housework and watch her little sister after school. Rebecca's way of coping with her overwhelmed parents was to try to be the perfect, responsible kid in order to gain her parents' love and approval. She thought that if she could only be good enough, they'd see her accomplishments and hard work. Instead, she was always reminded of her mistakes and shortcomings. She ended up feeling inferior no matter what she accomplished. Now, as an adult, she continues to push herself to work even harder and do even more, putting everyone else's needs in front of her own.

Did your parents display any of the traits of overwhelmed parents?

- ☐ They experienced chronic stressors or serious problems such as addiction or mental illness.
- ☐ They had either overly high expectations and rules or no expectations and rules.
- ☐ They were inconsistent.
- ☐ They were highly critical.
- ☐ They were impossible to please.
- ☐ They were moody, angry, or emotionally or physically abusive.
- ☐ They depended on their children to assume adult responsibilities such as household chores or to provide emotional support to their parents.
- ☐ They blamed the children for the family's problems.
- ☐ They were indifferent to their children's feelings and needs.
- ☐ They didn't provide affection (loving words, hugs, kisses).

The Connection Between Your Perfectionism and Your Childhood Experiences

There are differences between demanding, perfectionist, distracted, and overwhelmed parents, but they all share an inability to notice, understand, and value their children's feelings. Children experience this as a lack of interest in truly knowing them as people—their thoughts, feelings, dreams, and goals. Children parented by demanding, perfectionist, distracted, or overwhelmed parents learn that being perfect gets them attention and accolades or helps them avoid harsh punishment and criticism. Their self-worth (and sometimes their survival) depends on their ability to be the best, keep their parents happy, and create an illusion that they and their families are happy and well functioning. These children are always chasing external validation hoping it will finally make them feel good enough, and so these patterns continue into adulthood.

Did you have demanding, perfectionist, distracted, or overwhelmed parents? If so, what connections can you make between your perfectionism and how you were parented?

_____

_____

_____

_____

_____

Were you encouraged to be assertive, have your own opinions or goals, and try new things?

_____

_____

_____

_____

What happened when you performed well or achieved your goals (won an award, got good grades)?

_____

_____

_____

_____

_____

_____

_____

What happened when you made mistakes as a child? Were they seen as failures or learning opportunities? Were you forgiven or encouraged when you made a mistake or didn't achieve a goal?

_____

_____

_____

_____

_____

_____

_____

Perfectionist Messages from Culture and Media

As we grow up, we're influenced more and more by factors outside of our home environments. School and peers have a big impact on our development, as does the wider culture and world around us. So while you can trace your perfectionism back to your family of origin, you may find that the media as well as your church, schools, cultural customs, and community have also encouraged perfectionism.

America, for example, is built on the idea that hard work paves the way to success. This, in itself, isn't problematic; it can actually be motivating and hopeful. The problem is that valuing hard work has turned into valuing perfectionism and busyness and has encouraged the belief that success is for only the best and the brightest. Combine this with our emphasis on individualism, and we learn that (1) we have to be perfect and live up the images on our televisions and computers, and (2) we have to do it all on our own, because life's a competition, and only some of us can make it to the top.

In addition, technology has added to the pressures to do more and achieve more—and to look perfect while we're doing it. With technology, we can now work 24/7. And since we have all started carrying a little computer in our pockets, the line between work and time off has gotten really blurry. There are very few people who work nine to five, Monday through Friday anymore. Busyness has become a status symbol, and we're encouraged to work nonstop. Sometimes we trick ourselves into thinking that a flexible work schedule is to our advantage, but usually it just means we can work at home *and* at our place of business.

Technology also means we're saturated with images and messages from the media. We are spending more and more time watching television and YouTube, surfing the web, and perusing social media. These things all give us a specific image of who we're supposed to be, what we're supposed to look like, and what we're supposed to be doing. And that message is: You should be able to do everything, and you should make it look effortless. You should have a successful career, raise your kids with organic meals and enriching activities (never sticking them in front of the iPad), have a spotless house, take picture-perfect vacations to the beach, and love going to the gym.

Despite how far we think we've come, most American media outlets still feature tall, slim, Caucasian female models and tall, muscular, Caucasian male models. We grow up with this unattainable version of beauty. We are saturated with this message, making it easy to believe that if we don't look like those models, we aren't pretty enough or good enough. Dissatisfaction with one's body and the pressure to diet and be thin starts early. Research has shown that more than half of girls and one-third of boys aged six to eight think their ideal body would be significantly thinner than their actual body (Lowes and Tiggemann 2003). And one of the conclusions of Common Sense Media's 2015 research brief was that "there is strong documentation of unrealistic, idealized, stereotypical, and sexualized portrayals of body types. We also found evidence linking consumption of these media [movies, television, magazines, ads] with negative relationships to body image and behavior" (Pai and Schryver 2015, 31).

While all genders are certainly impacted by culture and media, women and girls seem to be particularly susceptible to perfectionism due to the way they're socialized. In Western cultures, girls are socialized as caretakers, to put the needs of others before their own, and to suppress their own feelings and goals in order to please others or keep the peace. Girls are taught to be neat and quiet and that being pretty and thin are measures of their worth.

Depending on your family's culture and religious traditions, there may be other teachings and models that encourage perfectionism and create unattainable expectations. In these situations, it's not just a family or parent, but a larger system that is teaching and reinforcing the notion that there is an exacting standard of worthiness and anything less is a failure or sign of inherent unworthiness.

For example, in her book *Battle Hymn of the Tiger Mother*, Amy Chua explains that traditional Chinese mothers leave no room for imperfections. They expect their children to be the best. Chua writes, "1) School work always comes first; 2) an A- is a bad grade; 3) your children must be two years ahead of their classmates in math;… 6) the only activities your children should be permitted to do are those in which they can eventually win a medal; and 7) that medal must be gold" (2011, 6).

My psychotherapy practice is in Silicon Valley, an area of the country that also breeds perfectionism and extremely high demands on children and adults to achieve and be at the top. People here have busy, high-pressure, and achievement-driven lifestyles. And they often fall into the comparison trap—thinking that everyone works at Apple or Google, drives a Tesla, and lives in a multimillion-dollar house. It's only natural that hardworking, middle-income folks feel like they're falling short. So while children living in Silicon Valley may get these messages from demanding or perfectionist parents, there's also a bigger cultural message that encourages working nonstop, outward signs of success, and productivity and achievement above all else.

What messages did you get (in words or actions) from your culture, religion, school, or media about success and needing to be perfect?

_____

_____

_____

_____

_____

_____

_____

Individual Traits

There may also be an innate temperament or sensitivities that predispose you to perfectionism. Researcher and psychotherapist Elaine Aron, PhD, identified that 15–20 percent of the population is naturally highly sensitive to and aware of the world around them. They feel things deeply and are more easily overwhelmed by highly stimulating environments. Some of the traits of highly sensitive people (HSPs) are also common among perfectionists, such as being excellent at avoiding and spotting errors and being extremely conscientious and adept at tasks that require accuracy, speed, and attention to detail (1998, 10). In her newsletter, Aron wrote, "HSPs tend to be perfectionists for two reasons. First, we don't like unpleasant surprises, such as criticisms, making a mistake, hurting others, or having something go very wrong. To avoid these, we try to plan, arrange, and do things perfectly…. Second, we tend to be perfectionists because we can envision how something could be done perfectly and aim for that" (2004).

A sensitive child can seem overly needy and hard to soothe to his or her caregivers. If you didn't have an attuned and responsive caregiver with the skills to create a sense of safety and secure attachment, the stage was set for you to feel insecure and have an unmet need for acceptance that fuels your perfectionism.

You and Your Family

These descriptions aren't true for every family. The roots of your perfectionism lie in the particular messages you got as a child from your parents, grandparents, teachers, culture, school, and religious groups, as well as the media. Take some time to answer the following questions to explore how your experiences have contributed to your perfectionism.

What did people expect of you as a child?

_____

_____

_____

_____

_____

_____

What happened when you met those expectations?

_____

_____

_____

_____

_____

_____

What were the consequences of not meeting expectations?

_____

_____

_____

_____

_____

_____

Why do you think you developed perfectionist traits?

_____

_____

_____

_____

_____

_____

Summary

In this chapter, we examined how and why perfectionism begins in childhood. You were able to consider whether your parents had a demanding, perfectionist, distracted, or overwhelmed parenting style and, if so, how that affected you—particularly how it contributed to your developing perfectionist traits to cope. In addition, we discussed the impact that the larger culture and media has in reinforcing unrealistically high expectations. And lastly, we considered that some perfectionist tendencies may be innate. You should now have a good idea of the factors that influenced the development of your perfectionist traits and of the fact that while they were instilled when you were impressionable and without healthier coping skills, they no longer work well for you. Now we're ready to move on to strategies for changing perfectionism. We will begin by gaining an understanding of the fears that underlie perfectionism and how to overcome them.

Chapter 4

From Fear to Courage

As people with unrealistically high standards, a need to please others, and all-or-nothing thinking, we have a particular set of fears that keep us stuck. Fear of failure, fear of criticism, and fear of rejection are commonly the driving forces beneath our perfectionism. Our perfectionism becomes a way for us to cope with and try to minimize anxiety-provoking thoughts and experiences. In this chapter, you'll identify which perfectionist fears are standing in your way and learn ways to determine whether your fears are accurate, and if they aren't, you'll learn ways to change your thinking so you can take advantage of all of life's opportunities and challenges and ultimately find the courage to embrace being imperfect.

How Your Brain Assesses Danger

Emotions are the body's way of telling us what it needs. Fear is a normal biological response meant to protect us from danger. Everyone has fears that guide decisions about what is safe and what isn't. However, for perfectionists, our warning systems are working overtime, alerting us to danger when it doesn't really exist. This is how we get trapped in our fears.

Fear is housed in the amygdala, the ancient, reptilian part of the brain that's responsible for the stress response you experience when faced with danger—the urge to fight, escape from, or freeze in the face of whatever it is that stresses you out. If you've ever encountered a small lizard or snake in your yard, it probably froze or ran off as soon as it sensed your presence. It instinctively knows that it can't win a fight with you, a much larger creature, so its best defense is to hold still and hope you don't notice or to scurry under a bush to safety. In much the same way, when your brain perceives danger, it immediately must decide if the best response is to run away, freeze (or play dead), or fight. And in making this decision, the amygdala acts on instinct rather than rational thought.

The brain has a negativity bias, which means we're more likely to think about what might go wrong than what might go right, and we're more likely to remember negative experiences than positive ones. For example, if you watched a news story about a plane crash that killed three hundred people and a heart-warming story about a seventy-five-year-old great-grandmother finally graduating from high school, you're more likely to remember the plane crash. The negativity bias was an evolutionary advantage that developed to help us stay alert and aware of potential dangers.

Fears, however, don't always give us an accurate assessment of danger. Sometimes the amygdala overreacts, and we feel afraid when there is actually little or no danger. This is particularly true when you've experienced a trauma or an upsetting event that you perceived as overwhelming and out of your control. After such an experience, we develop a heightened sensitivity and increased fear to protect ourselves from being hurt again. The amygdala becomes like a super-sensitive smoke detector that goes off every time you burn your toast. We're counting on it to alert us of actual danger, not something as minor as blackened toast. An overly sensitive smoke alarm, like an overly sensitive amygdala, makes it challenging to distinguish between real and perceived danger.

As perfectionists, our fears aren't so much of physical harm, but of emotional harm. From a biological standpoint, situations where we might be criticized, rejected, or embarrassed feel just as dangerous as a bull charging right at us. So the fear you feel when presenting a disastrous sales report to your boss is alerting you to the danger of being criticized and embarrassed, but your brain is likely exaggerating the danger in this situation.

When we let fear drive us, we miss out on opportunities and underestimate our ability to cope with setbacks. And because fear increases if we try to ignore it, the only way to get beyond our fears is to confront them. In the next sections, we'll work on recognizing our fears, challenging them to see if they're warranted, and learning to cope with uncomfortable situations and feelings. We'll do this in small chunks, so you can gradually increase your tolerance for anxiety-provoking situations.

Acknowledging Your Fears

Perfectionism can act as a shield that we use to keep people from seeing our imperfections and mistakes, which we're terrified to have revealed. Perfectionist fears tend to revolve around being inadequate and having other people find out, judge, and reject us because of our imperfections or deficits. We also have unrealistic expectations of ourselves—that we can and should be without fault, and that others will hold us to the same impossibly high standards that we have (and fail to meet). So we often hold people at a distance and only show them our praiseworthy parts, because we're afraid of what people will think if they find out that we failed to get the job we applied for or that we're having marital problems.

Fears also keep us from trying new things, making necessary changes, and embracing new opportunities. We're reluctant to try new things, because they involve the risk of making mistakes. Yet mistakes are inevitable; there is no way around them. It isn't possible to know how to do something perfectly the first time. But as perfectionists, we want to be perfect every time, so we spend a lot of time observing, studying, reading, rehearsing things in our heads, or sitting on the sidelines. We can choose to live life on the sidelines and avoid anything that may result in a mistake or failure, or we can work toward embracing mistakes and seeing them as normal. I like to think of mistakes as proof that you're fully living, trying new things, and being bold. The first step in moving past your perfectionist fears is to acknowledge them.

Which of these common perfectionist fears do you identify with?

☐ fear of failure   ☐ fear of not being liked

☐ fear of success   ☐ fear of being alone

☐ fear of rejection   ☐ fear of criticism

☐ fear of judgment   ☐ fear of trying new things

☐ fear of embarrassing yourself   ☐ fear of not being good enough

☐ fear of not being understood

How do these fears impact you? Do you keep people at a distance or miss out on opportunities because you're playing it safe?

_____

_____

_____

_____

_____

Now that you're more aware of your fears, we'll investigate whether they're accurate and helpful.

Are Your Fears Accurate?

Some fears are based on distorted thoughts. Cognitive behavioral therapy, pioneered by Albert Ellis, PhD, Aaron Beck, MD, and David Burns, MD, is based on the idea that your thoughts affect your feelings and behaviors. Specifically, when you become aware of and change your overly negative and unrealistic thoughts (often called "cognitive distortions," "negative automatic thoughts," or "irrational beliefs"), you can learn to feel better (less anxious and more hopeful), think more positively (speak to yourself with encouragement rather than criticism), and act in ways that help you reach your goals.

Perfectionist fears are made up of various cognitive distortions. These are some of the most common ones:

- **All-or-nothing thinking:** You see things as absolutes; there are no in-betweens.

- **Mind reading:** You assume others are thinking the same thing you are.

- **Double standard:** You hold yourself to a higher standard than everyone else.

- **Catastrophizing:** You expect the worst.

- **Labeling:** You label yourself negatively.

- **Magical thinking:** You think everything will be better when _____ (you're thinner, smarter, richer; when you get a new job, and so on).

- **Should statements:** You judge yourself and criticize yourself for what you should be doing.

Cognitive distortions are also common; we all think in counter-productive, unrealistic ways sometimes. Noticing our cognitive distortions is the first step to challenging them and replacing them with more realistic and helpful thoughts.

Noticing Your Cognitive Distortions

Use the chart on the next page to practice identifying some of the cognitive distortions behind your perfectionist thinking. This list of cognitive distortions is also at the back of the book in appendix A, for easy reference in the future.

Cognitive Distortion	Your Examples
All-or-nothing thinking You see things as absolutes, no in-betweens. Example: *I'm stupid.*	
Mind reading You assume others are thinking the same thing you are. Example: *I'm sure I didn't get the job because I'm too old.*	
Double standard You hold yourself to a higher standard than everyone else. Example: *I don't mind if your desk is a mess, but I have to keep mine neat and tidy.*	
Catastrophizing You expect the worst. Example: *I was late on the rent. I'm going to be evicted.*	
Labeling You label yourself negatively. Example: *I made a mistake. I'm a failure.*	
Magical thinking You think everything will be better when _____ (you're thinner, smarter, richer; when you get a new job). Example: *I'll meet Mr. Right once I lose twenty pounds.*	
Should Statements You judge yourself and criticize yourself for what you should be doing. Example: *I should run five miles every day before work.*	

For each of the fears you identified earlier in this chapter, try to recall a specific time you felt this way and record it below. I also want you to identify the distorted thoughts or beliefs that fuel the fear and the way you behaved in response to these thoughts and feelings. You may find it helpful to do this exercise at the end of each day for the next few weeks; if so, you can download additional copies of the "Noticing My Distorted Thoughts and Fears" worksheet from http://www .newharbinger.com/41535. This will help you gain awareness of how perfectionist fears impact your feelings and actions. Below is an example to help you get started.

Fear: *Fear of failure and not being good enough.*

Situation: *My sister got a promotion and a big raise.*

Underlying belief: *I'm not as smart as my sister. She's always more successful than me. I feel like I always take second place.*

Behavior: *I pretended to be happy for her and then felt ashamed of my jealousy. I yelled at my kids for making a mess, but mostly it was because I was in a bad mood about my sister's success. I stayed up late drafting a new proposal, hoping to impress my boss.*

Fear: _____

Situation: _____

_____

Underlying belief: _____

_____

_____

Behavior: _____

_____

_____

Fear: _____

Situation: _____

_____

Underlying belief: _____

_____

_____

Behavior: _____

_____

_____

Fear: _____

Situation: _____

_____

Underlying belief: _____

_____

_____

Behavior: _____

_____

_____

Challenging Your Fears

As I said earlier, fears aren't always an accurate assessment of danger, so we need to practice realistically assessing our fears to ensure that we're acting based on a judgment made with the prefrontal cortex rather than on the negativity bias of an overzealous amygdala.

Cognitive reframing is a four-step process that you can use to notice, challenge, and replace your distorted thoughts.

Step 1: Record your negative thoughts.

Step 2: Check for distortions. Do you see that your thoughts include cognitive distortions? The important thing is to recognize the distorted thoughts, so try not to overthink which types they are.

Step 3: Challenge the distortion. Look for evidence to support or refute this thought.

Asking yourself these questions can help you challenge cognitive distortions. This list can also be found in appendix B at the end of the book.

- How do I know if this thought is accurate?

- What evidence do I have to support this thought or belief?

- Do I have a trusted friend whom I can check out these thoughts with?

- Is this thought helpful?

- Are there other ways that I can think of this situation or myself?

- Am I blaming myself unnecessarily?

- What or who else contributed to this situation?

- Is it really in my control?

- Am I overgeneralizing?

- Am I making assumptions?

- What would I say to a friend in this situation?

- Can I look for shades of gray?

- Am I assuming the worst?

- Am I holding myself to an unreasonable or double standard?

- Are there exceptions to these absolutes (always, never)?

- Am I making this personal when it isn't?

- Who gets to decide what I have to or should do?

- Does this align with my values?

- Is this a realistic expectation?

- Am I expecting myself to be perfect?

Step 4: Replace distorted thoughts with more realistic thoughts.

Let's look at an example so you can see how you can use cognitive reframing to challenge your distorted fears and perfectionist thinking.

Ryan's Story

Ryan and his wife, Melissa, have a three-month-old baby daughter. Adjustment to parenthood has been rough for both. Melissa has postpartum depression, and it takes all her energy just to provide for her daughter's basic needs. Most days, she's gone back to bed by the time Ryan gets home. Ryan is overwhelmed and worried about his wife and daughter. When he gets home from work, he too is exhausted, but he focuses on getting his wife to shower and eat something. He then gets to work cooking, cleaning, doing the laundry, and feeding and playing with his daughter. Ryan and Melissa have close friends and parents who would be happy to give them a hand, but Ryan refuses to let anyone help. He hasn't told anyone that Melissa was diagnosed with postpartum depression or how much stress he's under. Whenever someone asks if she can drop off a casserole or pick up a few things from the store, he declines. Ryan's afraid he'll be judged. He thinks it's his job to take care of his family and asking for help proves that he's a failure and can't do it on his own. He's afraid of what people will think of Melissa's depression, and he imagines their friends would reject them if they knew. He's embarrassed to have anyone over because the house is a mess.

Step 1: Record your negative thoughts.

Ryan's negative thought: *Our friends and family will judge us for a messy house, mental health problems, and being overwhelmed.*

Step 2: Check for distortions.

Ryan's cognitive distortion: *This could be mind reading, a double standard, or catastrophizing.*

Step 3: Challenge the distortion.

Ryan's challenge: *My parents are supportive of my cousin who has depression. I've never known my friends to be judgmental about housekeeping or mental health. We helped Mary and Joe when their baby was born, and I didn't think any less of them because the lawn hadn't been mowed and laundry was piled up on the couch.*

Step 4: Replace distorted thoughts with more realistic thoughts.

Ryan's realistic thoughts: *Our friends and family will still love and accept us even if we're having problems and need help. I don't have to keep them at a distance and do it all myself.*

This was a very helpful exercise for Ryan. He can now see that asking for help isn't a sign of failure and that the risk of rejection or judgment is small. This sets the stage for Ryan to behave differently and courageously, say, by asking for help. It will still be challenging to behave differently after so many years, but bit by bit, you will find that you can let go of the fears and negative thoughts that have been holding you back. You can use the space below to practice replacing your fears and distorted thoughts with more accurate ones. (And if you find this process helpful, you can also download a "Challenging My Negative Thoughts" worksheet from http://www.newharbinger .com/41535 to work with other negative thoughts.)

Record your negative thoughts: _____

_____

_____

Check for cognitive distortions: _____

_____

Challenge the distortion: _____

_____

_____

Replace with more realistic thoughts: _____

_____

Record your negative thoughts: _____

_____

_____

Check for cognitive distortions: _____

_____

Challenge the distortion: _____

_____

_____

Replace with more realistic thoughts: _____

_____

Record your negative thoughts: _____

_____

_____

Check for cognitive distortions: _____

_____

Challenge the distortion: _____

_____

_____

Replace with more realistic thoughts: _____

_____

Courage in the Face of Perfectionism

When we get stuck in our perfectionist fears, we allow perfectionism to dictate what we can do and how we feel about ourselves. For most of us, these fears drastically limit us. Courage, however, is the antidote to our perfectionist fears. Being courageous in the face of perfectionism means we can take chances, tolerate mistakes, and live our lives fully.

Courage in the face of perfectionism takes many forms:

- self-acceptance

- asking for what you need

- sharing your mistakes rather than trying to hide them

- speaking your truth

- asking for help

- trying something new

- admitting when you're wrong

- speaking up for what you believe in

- allowing others to see your imperfections

Courage is like a muscle. The more you exercise it, the stronger it becomes. Practicing courage means repeatedly doing things that are just beyond your comfort zone. Most of us deal with change best when we do it incrementally. For example, if you are anxious speaking in public, I wouldn't suggest volunteering to speak in front of 1,500 colleagues at the next company-wide meeting. Instead, you might start with a smaller group, like your department or even your book club. Successfully speaking in front of your book club or presenting at a departmental staff meeting will build your confidence, and with practice, you'll have the courage to present to the entire company. The point is to challenge yourself just enough to feel discomfort, but not so much that you are overwhelmed and paralyze yourself.

You can't create the life you crave, whether it's financial success, a satisfying relationship, or high self-esteem, without taking risks. Growth is the essence of life. We are all changing constantly. When we embrace change and learn to value our mistakes as the stepping stones of self-improvement, we are moving toward our goals.

What does courage to be imperfect mean to you?

_____

_____

_____

_____

_____

Can you think of a time when you were courageous in the face of perfectionism and resisted being driven by fear and the need to achieve?

_____

_____

_____

_____

Summary

In this chapter, I asked you to identify your fears and consider how they are negatively impacting your life. We practiced noticing that fears are often based on distorted, or unrealistic, thoughts, and finding ways to challenge and replace them. This is a strategy based on cognitive behavioral therapy, which can be effective when practiced consistently. Over time, you'll be able to do this exercise in your head, but at the beginning, most people find it's most useful when it's done in writing. Now, we will move our focus to our self-critical thoughts and work on transforming them into more accepting and loving ways of thinking and acting toward ourselves.

Chapter 5

From Self-Criticism to Self-Compassion

As perfectionists, we're hard on ourselves, and this often takes the form of self-criticism. In this chapter, we'll examine how self-criticism is a barrier to accepting and caring for ourselves. I'm going to provide you with four strategies to help you move away from self-criticism and toward self-compassion: talking to yourself with compassion, cognitive reframing, practicing self-forgiveness, and focusing on your strengths. They all work synergistically, and you'll find they overlap nicely. But before we get to the strategies, let's first examine why we're so prone to self-criticism and how self-compassion can benefit us.

Self-Compassion Leads to Self-Acceptance

Self-compassion might sound strange, selfish, or soft, but it's a fairly simple concept that means you give yourself the same understanding and kindness that you might give a friend during a time of need. It includes talking to yourself kindly, forgiving yourself, taking care of your body, giving yourself comfort (like making time to savor a calming cup of tea at the end of a stressful day), and loving touch (such as giving yourself a hug or massage).

Kristin Neff, PhD, author of the book *Self-Compassion*, identifies three parts of self-compassion: (1) self-kindness rather than judgment or criticism in the face of struggle; (2) recognition of our common humanity, meaning that we feel connected to, not isolated from, others in our shared struggles; and (3) mindfulness, so that we are aware of our feelings, but not minimizing or exaggerating our pain (2011, 41). Using these three components, we can learn to treat ourselves with kindness and reap the rewards of self-compassion.

In this chapter, we'll practice ways of being kinder and gentler with ourselves using exercises inspired by Neff's work. We'll recognize that everyone has difficulties in life. My struggles might be different than yours, but you can be sure that no one has a problem-free life! And every one of us deserves compassion when we're going through a hard time, whether you forgot to pick up your son from swim practice or backed into another car in the parking lot. Understanding that our problems and flaws make us similar to others, not different from or less than they are, allows us to give ourselves the same kindness that we'd give a friend during a difficult time.

In order to give ourselves compassion, we need to first acknowledge that we're having a hard time. Noticing our own struggles can be surprisingly difficult. It requires us to mindfully pay attention to our thoughts and feelings and the physical sensations in our bodies. This could be thinking, *I'm having a rough day*, or *I'm overwhelmed by everything I have to do*, or noticing that you're irritable and physically exhausted. Only when we notice and accept our struggles can we respond with kindness and understanding. As perfectionists, we're particularly apt to deny our own shortcomings, struggles, and pain, because we view them as proof of our inadequacies. This is why it's especially important for us to work on transforming our self-criticism into self-compassion.

Perfectionists Never Feel Good Enough

We all talk to ourselves continuously. Most of this self-talk isn't even in our consciousness. We get so accustomed to our steady stream of thoughts that we don't pay attention to most of them. However, our unconscious thoughts are important, because they reflect what we believe about ourselves and influence our feelings and actions. Most perfectionists hold a core belief that we're not good enough, hence the need to constantly do more and be more. We create unrealistic expectations for ourselves, expectations that we'll be perfect; and when we inevitably fail to meet them, it serves as evidence that we're not as good as everyone else. Perfectionists meet this sense of failure with harsh self-criticism, which further reinforces our feelings of ineptitude.

Many of us find it easier to offer a kind gesture, encouraging word, or forgiveness to others than we do to ourselves. Sometimes we're truly quite awful to ourselves—saying and doing things to ourselves that we would never say or do to a friend. We subject ourselves to an unforgiving inner critic, unhealthy relationships, toxic substances, and self-punishment because we're convinced that we're different and inferior. We see ourselves as failures, idiots, careless, and lazy. We're quick to notice our faults and discount our positive qualities. And we criticize ourselves, because we think we deserve it. And because of our impossibly high standards, we see our faults as catastrophic. Hence, we worry that giving ourselves grace will lead to more failures and insecurities. We let our imperfections keep us disconnected rather than seeing the shared humanness in our imperfections.

Laurie is an example of a perfectionist who's very hard on herself. You'll notice that some of her negative self-talk is spoken out loud, and some are silent thoughts.

Laurie was plucking stray hairs from her chin one morning when her young daughter asked what she was doing. "I'm trying to make myself look presentable," she replied in a flustered tone. She examined herself in the mirror and said, "See all these wrinkles and these ugly black hairs on my chin? I'm old. No one wants to look at an old woman." Running late, as usual, she started yelling at her daughters to find their coats and backpacks and get in the car. "We're going to be late again!" she hollered. Minutes later, as she drove to work, she was berating herself: *I can't believe I lost my temper again. I said I was going to stop yelling. Why can't I ever plan ahead and get organized the night before? What's wrong with me?*

Can you relate to Laurie? Laurie is not only self-critical, but she sees her flaws as proof that she is different and "not enough." She imagines that other people have fewer wrinkles and chin hairs and are more organized and patient than she is. Laurie has homed in on her perceived shortcomings and wants to be more organized and patient, but she ends up criticizing herself, partly out of habit and also because she believes it will lead to changes in her behavior. However, self-criticism is unlikely to be an effective change strategy for Laurie or for you.

What do you say to yourself when you make a mistake, procrastinate, don't achieve your goals, lose your temper, don't live up to expectations, or feel not good enough, or when things don't go according to plan? Do you tend to be accepting and kind or harsh and judgmental?

_____

_____

_____

_____

If you're like most perfectionists, you tend to be self-critical. You may not be aware of the extent of your self-criticism, because you've grown accustomed to it and see it as normal. Or you may notice it but think it's deserved or even necessary. As we continue on, we'll work on both becoming more aware of our self-criticism and understanding that it's not warranted or helpful.

Isn't Self-Criticism Motivating?

Most perfectionists mistakenly believe that self-criticism will motivate them to excel or change and that meeting an error with compassion will only lead to poorer performance and more mistakes. If you made a mistake on your last sales report, you might say something critical to yourself: *I'm such an idiot. This is the worst report I've ever written.* This type of self-criticism might temporarily motivate you out of fear and shame, but at the same time, you're undermining your self-esteem and potentially increasing feelings of depression, anxiety, and shame. Ultimately, self-criticism makes us feel worse about ourselves, and it's hard to do better when we're yelling and calling ourselves derogatory names. Instead, imagine how it would feel if you responded to your mistake with compassion: *I feel embarrassed and frustrated about making this mistake, because I'm trying so hard to do well and impress my boss. I know I can do better next time. Maybe I need to get more sleep or finish my reports first thing in the morning when I'm fresh.*

As you can see from this example, self-compassion isn't self-indulgent. It's not giving ourselves a free pass when we screw up. We don't have to choose between accountability or compassion. Self-compassion allows us to give ourselves both the accountability and the understanding that we need to accept and improve ourselves, as well as the space in which to do so.

Self-compassionate people tend to be more motivated, because they are interested in learning from their mistakes. They can move on more quickly after a setback and set new goals instead of getting stuck in disappointment and self-reproach.

Over the years, has criticizing yourself made you feel better or worse about yourself?

_____

_____

How do you think acknowledging your struggles and responding to them with kindness could be motivating?

_____

_____

Support and encouragement help us to succeed. Some of that support may come from family, friends, or colleagues, but we can also provide ourselves with emotional support by replacing self-critical thoughts with kinder and more realistic self-talk. Self-compassion is a more effective and positive motivator than self-criticism. So, now that we've identified some of the benefits of self-compassion, we'll work on practicing it.

Talk to Yourself with Compassion

Talking to yourself kindly is an important form of self-compassion and a natural antidote to self-criticism. The following exercise will help you identify self-critical thoughts, recognize that you aren't alone in your failures and imperfections, and offer yourself compassion. Use the space below to give it a try, and then continue to practice using compassionate self-talk at least once a day. The more you practice, the more natural it will feel.

Identify a situation in which you were self-critical.

Sample response: *I was late picking up my daughter from preschool. She was the last child there, and her teacher looked annoyed with me. I told myself, "I'm the worst mom. Why can't you get anything right?"*

_____

_____

_____

_____

_____

_____

What is the pain you're experiencing?

Sample response: *I felt like a failure as a mom. I was embarrassed and ashamed. I was sad about upsetting my daughter and making the teacher stay late.*

_____

_____

_____

_____

_____

_____

Are you the only human who has ever made this type of mistake? How do you know?

Sample response: *No, my husband has been late before. And I've heard Sara say that it's really hard for her to pick up Jack by six.*

_____

_____

_____

_____

_____

_____

Now that you're aware of your pain and see that you aren't the only one who has done these things (hurt someone, failed, made a mistake, and so on), what would you say to someone else who is experiencing this pain?

Sample response: *You're not a bad mom just because you were late. You take really good care of your daughter and work hard all day to provide for her. I know you're doing the best you can.*

_____

_____

_____

_____

_____

_____

Now try giving yourself the same compassionate response that you'd give a friend.

Sample response: *Sharon, you're not a bad mom just because you were late. You take really good care of your daughter and work hard all day to provide for her. You're doing the best you can.*

_____

_____

_____

_____

_____

_____

_____

How does it feel to give yourself compassion in a difficult time?

_____

_____

_____

_____

_____

_____

_____

_____

Cognitive Reframing

As we did in the previous chapter on challenging our fears, we're going to use cognitive reframing to change exaggerated or inaccurate negative thoughts (cognitive distortions) about ourselves. Self-criticism becomes an automatic response for most of us. In fact, a lot of our thoughts aren't in our conscious awareness. They're like elevator music humming in the background, setting the tone, without us even realizing it. In this case, the tone is critical, negative, and pessimistic. We want to replace this with more balanced and realistic thoughts. So, to begin to change this, we want to become more aware of our self-critical thoughts.

Noticing Self-Criticism

The first step in changing negative thoughts—what's often called "negative self-talk"—is to get really clear about the negative things we're saying to ourselves.

Over the next several days or weeks, record the negative thoughts you have about yourself. You can start with the following chart (which you can also download as a worksheet, "Noticing Self-Criticism," from http://www.newharbinger.com/41535), but you may find it more convenient to do it on a notepad you carry with you, on a journaling app, or as a written or voice memo on your phone. You may be surprised at how often you're being self-critical.

Be on the lookout for the words *always*, *never*, and *should*. They're often signs that criticism is at work. You may also find it helpful to refer to the list of cognitive distortions at the end of the book (appendix A).

Day and time	Situation	Negative self-talk
Monday, 8:30 a.m.	Spilled my cup of coffee.	I'm so clumsy. Now I'm going to be late.

Challenging Self-Criticism

We start the process of changing our negative thoughts by looking for evidence to either support or refute our negative beliefs about ourselves. The questions we used in the previous chapter (you can find a copy in appendix B) can be helpful in exploring whether your thinking is accurate.

It's important to go through the step of challenging your negative self-talk before replacing it with something more positive, because it feels phony to simply say positive things to ourselves if we don't believe them.

Completing this chart (which is also available in downloadable format, "Challenging Self-Criticism," from http://www.newharbinger.com/41535) will help you practice identifying, challenging, and changing your negative self-talk.

Negative self-talk	Challenge	Realistic or positive self-talk
I'm so clumsy.	I spilled my coffee because I was in a rush. I don't do this every day. It's not fair to label myself "clumsy." I don't think I'm clumsier than other people.	I was in a rush. Spilling coffee doesn't make me clumsy. This isn't worth criticizing myself over.
I'm sure Megan's going to get the promotion. She's much smarter and prettier than I am.	I don't know who's going to get the promotion. I know I've had excellent performance reviews the past two years, and my manager sent me that nice e-mail after my last presentation. I'm assuming the worst.	I've worked hard and done my best. That's all I can expect of myself. Maybe I'll get the promotion, maybe I won't—either way, I'm still a good employee and a good person.

Changing our self-talk is an important part of moving from self-criticism to self-compassion. However, sometimes our self-criticism is deeply lodged as a result of something we feel very badly about. Self-forgiveness is an approach that can be helpful in addition to cognitive reframing.

Practice Self-Forgiveness

Because we demand a lot of ourselves and are constantly disappointed in our imperfect performance and behavior, we tend to hold on to our mistakes and continue to castigate ourselves for things that we did wrong. You might be continuing to punish yourself for yelling at your children, like Laurie did, or for causing a car accident. Mistakes become a heavy load to bear for perfectionists, because we severely (and sometimes inappropriately) blame ourselves, and our list of wrongs and mistakes only grows unless we take steps to accept our mistakes and imperfections and forgive ourselves.

Forgiveness is a way of giving ourselves compassion and accepting our mistakes; it normalizes them. Forgiveness recognizes our shared humanity—we all make mistakes and have regrets, and no one deserves to be perpetually criticized for them.

However, our perfectionism, a reflection of our feelings of inadequacy, makes it hard for us to forgive ourselves, and self-criticism is a barrier to self-forgiveness. But beating ourselves up for our imperfections and mistakes does not ultimately serve us well—or those that we may have hurt. The best way to make things right and feel at peace is to acknowledge and take responsibility for our mistakes, apologize or repair any damage caused, and commit ourselves to learning from them. It's much harder to do these things when we're bogged down with self-loathing or depression than when we're practicing self-compassion.

Forgiving ourselves doesn't mean we disregard our mistakes or excuse our poor choices. On the contrary, forgiveness requires that we take responsibility for our actions and believe that compassion will allow us to move forward toward better choices.

Self-forgiveness is more of a process than an event. It's something that you will practice over and over again in order to gradually release your self-criticism and the belief that you deserve to be punished for your imperfections. Self-forgiveness happens when—bit by bit—we believe that we truly did the best we could and understand why we made the choices that we did. Hindsight really is twenty-twenty, which is why it's completely unfair to judge our past selves with the knowledge and skills we have now. Remember: "When we know better, we do better."

If you're highly self-critical and holding on to past mistakes, you can work toward self-forgiveness with the following exercises: re-do a regret, forgiveness affirmation, and take positive action. Each one can be a part of the process of self-forgiveness.

Re-Do a Regret

We can't, of course, travel back in time and do things differently. But it can still help to think about what we would have done differently and give ourselves compassion; this helps us learn from our mistakes and keep things in perspective.

Think of a situation that you're struggling to forgive yourself for, something you're feeling shame, regret, hurt, or anger about. Describe what happened below.

_____

_____

_____

_____

_____

_____

What can you say to your past self to offer understanding and compassion during that situation or experience?

_____

_____

_____

_____

_____

_____

If you could do it over, what would you do differently?

_____

_____

_____

_____

_____

_____

_____

See if you can implement what you just described the next time you're in a similar situation.

Forgiveness Affirmation

An affirmation can create a positive mindset and energy that can help you start to think about yourself differently and then, ultimately, treat yourself differently. For example, Laurie used a forgiveness affirmation to stop beating herself up about losing her temper with her daughters during times of stress and to remain focused on her goal of being less reactive and self-critical.

Laurie's forgiveness affirmation:

> I forgive myself for _yelling at the girls._ I release myself from _feeling guilty and like a terrible mother and person._ I accept that I'm human and I make mistakes. Now, I would do things differently, but I did the best I could at the time, and I forgive myself for my mistakes.

You can use this formula for your self-forgiveness affirmation or you can modify it as needed.

> I forgive myself for _____. I release myself from _____. I accept that I'm human and I make mistakes. Now, I would do things differently, but I did the best I could at the time, and I forgive myself for my mistakes.

Or write your own personal forgiveness affirmation:

_____

_____

_____

Try repeating your affirmation every morning and every evening. See how it feels. You can change the affirmation to language that speaks to your specific pain and regret. Make it meaningful to you.

Take Positive Action

It's important that we acknowledge our mistakes—not so we can punish ourselves for them, but so we can learn from them and accept our imperfections. Sometimes our mistakes also negatively impact others, and this can be an especially painful reminder of our imperfections. However, getting stuck in rumination and regret doesn't help anyone. We can try to make the best of a mistake by learning from it, giving an apology or making amends to those who were hurt, or by doing something good in the world.

Often, part of releasing ourselves from regret is giving an apology and making amends. A quality apology has three parts: (1) taking responsibility for our actions and the impact, (2) showing regret, and (3) offering to fix things. Here's an example: "Isaiah, I'm sorry I took credit for your idea during the customer meeting. That was wrong. I see now that it made you look unprepared and incompetent in front of our customer. I'd like to talk to our supervisor and the customer to take responsibility for my wrongdoing and give you full credit for the idea."

Think of a situation in which you did something you wish you could apologize for. Practice writing an apology that takes responsibility, shows regret, and offers a repair.

_____

_____

_____

_____

_____

Sometimes the person you need to apologize to is you. If you've been degrading yourself, cursing at yourself, and holding yourself hostage emotionally, it can be a powerful exercise to forgive yourself for being mean and unnecessarily harsh with yourself. You would expect an apology if someone else treated you this way, so why not give yourself an apology? Jacie's story is an example of self-forgiveness.

Jacie's Story

Years after her mother died, Jacie continued to beat herself up for not getting to her mother's bedside in time to say goodbye. Her siblings had all been there to comfort their mother and hold her hand as she died. Jacie felt like an awful daughter. Jacie's apology to herself went like this: "I'm sorry that I've guilted you and said you were a bad daughter. I'm sorry that I've let you focus on this regret and let it color your memories of Mom and our relationship. That wasn't fair. I want to be kind to you going forward and offer you understanding and compassion when you're suffering."

Try writing an apology to yourself for being self-critical and harsh.

_____

_____

_____

_____

_____

_____

Sometimes an apology isn't possible and we can't make amends to the injured party. This doesn't mean we are doomed to a lifetime of regret and self-criticism. We can still lessen the negative impact by taking positive action in the world. In Jacie's case, she did apologize to herself, but she still felt unsettled. She finally started to feel better when she began a practice of sending sympathy cards with a heartfelt message to parishioners in her church when a loved one died. This was a small but meaningful way that Jacie could help others.

Doing something positive in the world doesn't need to be time-consuming or costly. You can simply do something small, like bringing in your elderly neighbor's trash cans, as a way to counter your negative and self-critical perfectionist beliefs, make amends, and focus on how you can make the world a better place.

What are some simple ways that you can take positive action in the world?

_____

_____

_____

_____

_____

_____

_____

Focus on Your Strengths

You're probably hyperaware of your faults and shortcomings but unaware of or quick to dismiss your strengths and positive personality traits. Perfectionism gives us an inaccurate perception of ourselves. We become internally focused on our imperfections and failures, which we try to keep hidden from everyone else. This creates an inaccurate self-assessment, which contributes to our tendency to self-criticize.

Identifying Your Strengths

We all have strengths and weaknesses, but as perfectionists, we tend to magnify our weaknesses and ignore our strengths. It's not realistic to expect ourselves to know everything, excel at everything, and win every competition. And it's not fair to discount our strengths and positive attributes. We've talked about ways to begin to accept our weaknesses and mistakes, but we also need to rebalance our thinking by recognizing our strengths.

As you work on identifying your strengths, remember that strengths are not the same as achievements. Achievements have their place, but they are only part of who you are. We want to tap into the inner character strengths, personality traits, and positive attributes that make you special.

You can use this list of strengths to help you get started.

- creative
- determined
- patient
- confident
- kind
- energetic
- focused
- gracious
- humorous
- spiritual
- a team player
- independent
- playful

- hardworking
- attentive to detail
- honest
- open-minded
- able to keep things in perspective
- organized
- practical
- disciplined
- brave
- loyal
- generous
- responsible
- thoughtful

- adaptable
- consistent
- spontaneous
- positive
- authentic
- a lifelong learner
- hopeful
- appreciative of the small things
- curious
- self-aware
- empathetic
- prudent

What strengths do you see in yourself? (List at least five.)

_____

_____

_____

_____

_____

If you have trouble with this exercise, try asking yourself these questions.

What strengths have contributed to your successes?

_____

_____

What activities or roles do you enjoy?

_____

_____

Which of your personality traits bring you joy?

_____

_____

Which of your personality traits reflect your values?

_____

_____

You can also ask two or three close friends, family members, or colleagues about your strengths. Sometimes others see things that we don't recognize in ourselves.

What strengths do your friends and family see in you? In what ways do they value you for what you do—and who you are?

_____

_____

_____

_____

_____

Give and Accept Compliments

Giving ourselves compliments and accepting them from others is another way we can act in a loving way toward ourselves. Many people tend to disregard compliments. We shrug them off, not wanting people to think we're narcissistic or conceited. However, most compliments are given freely with an open heart. They are intended to focus on the positive and to brighten your day. Graciously accepting a compliment brings joy to both the giver and the receiver.

Write down some compliments that you've received in the past few weeks. If none come to mind, be on the lookout for them for the next few days, and write them down when you receive them.

_____

_____

_____

_____

_____

How do you typically respond to compliments?

_____

_____

_____

_____

_____

_____

When you receive a compliment, remind yourself that someone else has recognized something positive about you and wanted to let you know. Let it soak in. If you don't entirely believe what the other person's telling you, perhaps mull it over and look for some truth in it. And even if you don't completely agree with the compliment, try receiving it as a loving gesture—an expression of his or her care for you. You might respond by saying, "thank you," "thanks for noticing," "I appreciate your kindness," or "yes, I'm really happy about that, too."

What response or responses to compliments feel right to you?

_____

_____

Now we're going to practice giving *ourselves* compliments. As perfectionists, we already tend to base our value on our achievements, so for this exercise, try to focus on your strengths, things that matter to you (not things that you did to please others), and challenges you've overcome, as well as the self-improvement, effort, or progress you've made. This is another place to watch that you don't get caught up in all-or-nothing thinking. It's totally valid to give yourself a virtual gold star for prepping your lunches for the week on Sunday night, even if you didn't manage to do it last week. These compliments are about what's happening right now.

Try to record at least one positive thing about yourself per day and then write it as a compliment. To reinforce your strengths and efforts, it's great to come back to this list and reread it, say the compliments out loud, or write them on sticky notes that you stick on your mirror or computer for extra reinforcement. (For a worksheet version of this exercise, "Give Yourself a Compliment," that you can print out and post, visit http://www.newharbinger.com/41535.)

Date	Positive quality or effort	Compliment
Sunday	*Stayed calm while I taught my sixteen-year-old to drive, even though inside I was super anxious.*	*Sharon, I'm really proud of you for staying calm and not showing Sophie how anxious you were about her driving.*

After you've spent some time practicing self-compassion and giving yourself compliments, be sure to look for opportunities to compliment yourself for using compassionate self-talk and forgiveness instead of self-criticism.

Summary

We can change self-critical patterns by incorporating compassionate self-talk, cognitive reframing, forgiveness, and focusing on strengths into our daily routines. These strategies will help you to notice when you're struggling and give you the love and understanding that you need and deserve. Next, we will be tackling the challenge of procrastination, which can also lead to self-criticism and diminished self-esteem. We'll look at why we procrastinate, practical approaches for increasing motivation, and ways to be kind to ourselves when we fall prey to procrastination.

Chapter 6

From Procrastinating to Getting Things Done

We've all experienced procrastination—that knowledge that you *should* be doing something productive, but instead of starting the laundry, you've spent the last hour watching one YouTube video after another. Because of our impossibly high standards, we perfectionists tend to be harder on ourselves than most people when we procrastinate. In this chapter, we're going to take a closer look at how overwhelm, fear, and perfectionist thinking contribute to procrastination and how to break the cycle by changing our thoughts and behaviors.

Why We Procrastinate

Some people are surprised that perfectionists procrastinate, because we're generally such workhorses. It's true that perfectionists will not take a missed deadline or sloppy work lightly, but we aren't immune to the overwhelm, fear, and negative thinking that fuel procrastination.

Overwhelm

One reason for procrastination is that we become overwhelmed with the multitude of complex tasks we've taken on. If you have a hard time saying no to new projects or added responsibilities and are constantly trying to prove yourself, you've probably taken on more work (housework, volunteer work, side hustles) and pursued more goals than the average person. You might pride yourself on cleaning the whole house three nights a week in addition to your sixty-hour-a-week work schedule. Or you might find yourself shooting off e-mails as you're standing on the sidelines at your kid's soccer practice, desperate to keep tabs on the latest major project even as you try to be the perfect parent cheering your son on. As a result of this drive to extend yourself and do everything you possibly can, you may get burned-out and overwhelmed.

Perfectionism increases the pressure and overwhelm, because we don't just expect ourselves to do all the things we take on; we expect ourselves to do them perfectly and effortlessly. Sometimes we experience analysis paralysis—an inability to make decisions or take action because we're overwhelmed by the number of choices we have and the need for every action we take to be just right.

Are there goals, projects, deadlines, or responsibilities that feel overwhelming right now? If so, write them down to help clarify what feels stressful.

_____

_____

_____

_____

_____

_____

Perfectionist Thinking

Overwhelm isn't the only reason we procrastinate. The need to do things flawlessly adds tons of extra pressure to every task. So projects don't get started and work doesn't get done because of our fear of not doing them perfectly. And sometimes it feels safer to not act—to procrastinate.

Perfectionist thoughts are harsh, all-or-nothing messages that underlie our belief that imperfections are the same as failures, inadequacies, and unworthiness. Perfectionist thinking that contributes to procrastination includes many different kinds of thoughts:

- If it's not perfect, it's not worth doing.

- If it's this hard, I must be stupid.

- What if I mess up?

- I'll probably embarrass myself.

- Mistakes are unacceptable.

- I'm not good at _____.

- I have to do everything myself; I'm the only one who can do this correctly.

Perfectionist thinking impedes our ability to try new things, take chances, and stretch ourselves. As we've discussed previously, perfectionist thinking is based on cognitive distortions or false information and assumptions. It plays on our fears and increases our feelings of overwhelm and the pressure to perform, which leads to avoidance and procrastination.

Notice and record the perfectionist thoughts you have that may contribute to avoidance and procrastination.

_____

_____

_____

_____

_____

Fear

As we discussed in chapter 5, fear of failure, rejection, and criticism can stand in the way of acting. These fears are magnified by perfectionist thinking that tells us that mistakes are catastrophic. You can avoid failure, rejection, and criticism by procrastinating or avoiding certain tasks and situations altogether. However, this only magnifies your fears and increases the anxiety and stress that you feel about having incomplete projects or unmet goals.

What are some things that you procrastinate doing because you're afraid of doing them imperfectly or being criticized?

_____

_____

_____

_____

_____

Does procrastination make you feel more stressed and increase your fears of failure, rejection, and criticism? Can you think of a time that this happened?

_____

_____

_____

_____

_____

Why Procrastination Is a Problem

Some procrastination is normal; but procrastination does cause problems, especially if you do it regularly. Procrastination doesn't just get in the way of us achieving our goals. Procrastination can also cause us to miss out on opportunities, waste time, and feel even more stressed and overwhelmed.

Missed Opportunities

Procrastination can cause us to miss out on opportunities to learn, experience new things, meet new people, have fun, advance in our career, and challenge ourselves. Ty's story is an example of how procrastination can lead to missed opportunities.

Ty's Story

Ty is an avid singer and songwriter. He loves to sing for his family, but he's never performed in public. When his brother-in-law invited him to perform at a local open mic night, it piqued his interest, and he started thinking about signing up. Naturally, Ty was nervous about the prospect of his first public performance, so he put off signing up. Two days passed, then a third. He kept telling himself he'd do it, but instead of signing up and practicing for the show, he stayed late at work, got a haircut, took his car in for service, and started painting his porch. The deadline came and went, and Ty told his brother-in-law that he was just too busy.

Has this ever happened to you? You wanted to do something, but you put it off, stalled, made excuses, and didn't make a decision until the opportunity had passed you by. Maybe it was a job you didn't apply for, a relationship that you didn't pursue, a trip you didn't take, an appointment you never scheduled, or a party you didn't attend.

What opportunities have you missed by procrastinating or getting stuck in analysis paralysis?

Wasted Time

When we're avoiding something, we often end up wasting time doing things that don't really matter or don't benefit us. For example, if you really want to spend an hour watching YouTube, it's not necessarily a waste of time. When we allow ourselves simple pleasures and enjoy them, they are restorative and bring us joy. But when you watch YouTube to avoid starting the laundry, it probably isn't giving you the same boost of happiness. Often, you'll end up criticizing yourself for the things you procrastinated on.

How does procrastination lead to wasted time for you?

_____

_____

_____

_____

_____

Stress, Overwhelm, and Self-Criticism

Putting things off generally increases anxiety. Even if you're distracting yourself, it can be hard to fully relax when you still haven't made that difficult phone call to your boss. The unfinished task nags at you and continues to stress you out for as long as you postpone it. In contrast, most people feel relief when they complete a difficult task, even if it didn't go well. To further understand the connection between stress and procrastination, let's take a look at Madison's experience.

Madison's Story

Madison is a new case manager for a maternal mental health program, and all of her clients adore her. She's totally in touch with their feelings and personal needs; she helps them navigate their insurance benefits, goes above and beyond to provide them with resources, and is on call for their needs 24/7. This sounds like stellar job performance, but Madison procrastinates other essential job responsibilities. She puts off writing required notes in the clients' charts after each interaction and delays entering her billing, which is supposed to be done within forty-eight hours of her client meetings, because these are tedious tasks and because she's anxious about making a mistake. She has over a month's worth of paperwork to do, which has resulted in her being given a written warning. Her anxiety and stress have skyrocketed. The task has become so big and overwhelming that she can't get herself to even start. Madison has known for some time that she isn't meeting her employer's standards or her own expectations, which made her become frustrated with herself. She sits at her computer and thinks, _Just do it, you idiot. You're going to get fired if you don't do your paperwork._ This self-criticism initially got Madison to sit down and start on the paperwork, but she found herself getting more discouraged and self-critical and ultimately falling even further behind.

I can relate to Madison's and Ty's experiences with procrastination, and I imagine you can too. Avoidance and procrastination are common strategies that perfectionists use to deal with overwhelming and anxiety-provoking tasks. As a result, we miss out on opportunities, or we create even more stress by not doing things that really need to be done.

How does procrastinating create more stress, overwhelm, and negative feelings for you?

_____

_____

_____

_____

_____

Now that we've identified the problems caused by procrastination, let's begin to change the thinking patterns and behaviors that support procrastination.

Challenge Your Perfectionist Thinking

As we've discussed in previous chapters, our perfectionist thinking is based on inaccurate and distorted beliefs and assumptions. We can learn to be more aware of how perfectionist thinking leads to procrastination, challenge the underlying distortions, and replace them with more realistic ones. This will help us reduce procrastination.

Reframe Negative Perceptions

The way we think about a task creates our feelings about it, and how we feel about the task then leads us to either do it or procrastinate. Most likely you're giving yourself negative, defeatist messages about the tasks you're avoiding without even realizing it. These messages may sound like one of these:

- *This is so hard. I can't do this.*

- *I hate doing my taxes. I'm sure I'm doing them all wrong.*

- *I know I have to do this, but I really don't want to—it's just so boring.*

This negative thinking contributes to procrastination, which, in turn, creates more negative self-talk. We start beating ourselves up for not being productive or perfect, calling ourselves "lazy" or a "failure," which further decreases our motivation. We can't possibly be our best selves and do our best work when we call ourselves disparaging names.

We can get out of this negative cycle by shifting our thinking from focusing on the negative to acknowledging the positives. This could sound like: *This is a challenge, but I actually like learning new things!* or *Taxes aren't my favorite thing to do, but I know that I'm capable of figuring them out, and it feels so good when they're done.*

Be on the lookout for these cues that you're thinking negatively about a task, and add your own cues to the list:

- It's boring.

- It's hard.

- I hate this.

- It's not important.

- It will take too long.

- I don't know how to do it.

- I might fail.

- _____

- _____

Now, practice cognitive reframing by completing the following table with the realistic or encouraging self-talk statements you might use for your most common negative thoughts.

Negative self-talk	Realistic or encouraging self-talk
I hate mowing the lawn.	*It only takes thirty minutes. It's not that bad. I can listen to music while I do it to make it go by faster.*

Look for Partial Successes

Procrastination can lead us to not starting or finishing things. If we procrastinate long enough, it becomes impossible to do time-sensitive things like going to an exercise class or registering for an event. Sometimes we use procrastination to get out of doing things we think are unpleasant. My kids quickly figured out that if they procrastinate washing the dishes long enough, there's a good chance I'll end up doing them!

It's tempting to not start things when we think we can't do them perfectly. This type of all-or-nothing thinking makes it hard to see that often there is still a benefit in doing part of a task or project or that some things don't need to be done to exceptionally high standards. Let's say I decided to go to the gym every morning before work, but I dawdled too long over my morning coffee, and now I don't have time to go to the spin class that I like. If I let my perfectionist thinking dictate, I'd say, "It's too late now. I guess I can't exercise today." Alternatively, I could say, "Well, I missed my spin class, but I could still go walking for twenty minutes before work." My perfectionist self would be inclined to see this as a failure, because I didn't meet my commitment to go to the spin class and the walk wasn't as good of a workout. A more compassionate and accepting way to think about this—one that will keep me from falling into disappointment and procrastination in the future—is as a partial success.

It's very hard to motivate ourselves when we frame things only as "success" or "failure." So much of life is truly shades of gray. When we set unrealistic expectations and believe we are failures (or lazy or stupid) when we don't perform flawlessly, it's easier to not do things at all. Going for a short walk wasn't my ideal workout, but it still provided me with health benefits. The same is true for journaling, following a budget, meditating, healthy eating, and really any positive activity we're trying to do. In other words, we don't have to do things perfectly for them to have value.

Here's another example of a partial success. Madison set a goal to spend one extra hour at the office every day to catch up on her paperwork, but she didn't achieve this goal. She skipped one day completely and worked on her paperwork for only forty minutes another day. Instead of considering this a failure, Madison could see it as a partial success, because the time she did put in allowed her to complete the overdue paperwork for two of her clients. She now feels encouraged that she can manage the paperwork and succeed at her job. She didn't follow her plan perfectly, but there was a positive result. Like Madison, when we measure by progress rather than perfection, we're more motivated and energized to continue. When we see every imperfection as a failure, we're more likely to give up.

What's an example from your life of how doing some is better than doing none, as a partial success?

_____

_____

_____

_____

_____

In addition to challenging the perfectionist thinking that drives you to procrastinate, there are strategies you can use to make the tasks you procrastinate on easier to handle. We'll explore some of these techniques in the next section.

Decrease Overwhelm, Increase Motivation

Now I'm going to share five strategies to decrease procrastination by lessening the feelings of overwhelm that can stop you in your tracks and by increasing your motivation for the things you find difficult: the five-minute rule, breaking tasks down, doing the hardest thing first, accepting imperfection, and minimizing distractions. I encourage you to try each of the strategies over the course of several weeks to see which ones are the most effective for you.

The Five-Minute Rule

Getting started is usually the hardest part of any task, but often the task isn't as difficult, unpleasant, or time-consuming as we've made it out to be in our minds. The five-minute rule works by committing to do something for just five minutes—and then you can quit if you want. So if you've got three boxes of old bank statements, bills, and taxes that you need to organize, just commit yourself to working on it for five minutes today. Most things are tolerable for five minutes, and psychologically, it's much easier to motivate yourself for five minutes of filing than for five hours. If you get some momentum and end up doing more, great! Often, things aren't so bad once we've gotten going; it's just getting started that's the hard part. And even if you don't continue, you'll still be five minutes ahead.

For the next few weeks, try the five-minute rule for some of the tasks you procrastinate on. You can use this chart to help you determine whether the five-minute rule is a helpful strategy for you. I encourage you to try it on several different tasks.

Task	How did you feel about the task before you began?	How long did you actually spend on the task?	Was the five-minute rule helpful in getting started?	How did you feel after working on the task for at least five minutes?
Researching preschools for my son.	Overwhelmed by the amount of work; anxious about making the right choice.	Fifteen minutes.	Yes, knowing I could quit after five minutes took some of the pressure off.	I felt relieved and optimistic. I got organized and identified a couple schools to call.

Break It Down

Breaking complex or large tasks into manageable pieces is a commonly used productivity strategy that you probably already use. It's much easier to do anything that takes sustained focus, whether it's finding a new job or composing a song, when you break it down into bite-sized pieces. It's also motivating to set goals that are achievable. It's discouraging to see "get a new job" on your list of goals week after week. By contrast, it's hopeful and motivating when you see pieces of this goal, such as "update resume" and "set up networking lunch with Helen," crossed off your list. You can use the exercise below, the Task Map, to break down a project. (For a downloadable version of this worksheet, called "Task Map," that you can use to break down any task, visit http://www .newharbinger.com/41535.)

Try creating a visual map of the steps to accomplish your goal. For bigger projects, just keep adding more tasks and sub-tasks. When you're ready to begin, focus on just one sub-task at a time.

Goal: _____

Task 1: _____

    Task 1.1: _____

    Task 1.2: _____

Task 2: _____

    Task 2.1: _____

    Task 2.2: _____

Task 3: _____

    Task 3.1: _____

    Task 3.2: _____

Do the Hardest Thing First

Most people are inclined to do the easiest thing on their to-do list first. There's something very satisfying about checking something off (no matter how small). So we make a beeline for the quickest, easiest task, like reading and replying to e-mail, and do that first. However, this probably isn't our most important chore or task, so we can end up using our optimal energy and focus on something that doesn't require it and then potentially having less to give to our most challenging or important projects.

The idea behind starting with the hardest thing is that you're probably at your best—the most focused and energized—early in the day or at the outset of a project. The more you put off the hardest task, the harder it will seem, and the less likely you are to do it. Getting the most painful tasks done first and ending the day with the easier or more enjoyable ones can also contribute to a greater sense of happiness and success. If you're unsure about applying this to your entire to-do list, try using it for a multipart project, such as cleaning your house.

Look at your to-do list or write one below. Rank order the items from most challenging or unpleasant to easiest or most enjoyable.

1. _____

2. _____

3. _____

4. _____

5. _____

6. _____

7. _____

8. _____

9. _____

10. _____

Once you have your ranked list, try using it to complete the tasks you hoped to finish.

Was it helpful to do the hardest things first? Notice whether doing the hardest things first increased your productivity and satisfaction. Will this be a useful strategy for you?

_____

_____

_____

Accept Imperfection

We can also decrease our feelings of overwhelm by reducing the pressure we put on ourselves to be faultless. For many tasks, I find the mantra "done is better than perfect" helpful, because often trying to do something perfectly means it doesn't get done or I spend far too much time on a task relative to its importance. I could wash and shine my car to perfection or edit a blog post endlessly, but it wouldn't be a good use of my time, as neither of these things needs to be flawless. It can be hard to choose between done and perfect, because we really want both, but this is often not realistic or practical. Ultimately, it's more fulfilling to plan and host an imperfect graduation party for your son than to not have one at all. It's simply unrealistic to expect that you can get all the moving parts of a party—decorations, tableware, invitations, food, and drinks—all put together perfectly.

In the space below, come up with your own mantra to accept imperfection. You can try adopting my mantra or write your own.

_____

_____

Once you have a mantra, you can reinforce it by writing it on some sticky notes you put around your house, or you can make a screen saver for your computer or phone with the mantra prominently displayed.

Certainly, telling yourself to let go and accept imperfection is one thing; actually doing this is quite another. But we can apply a "good enough" standard to many tasks without any negative consequences except our own initial discomfort, which will lessen the more we do it. We can move toward accepting imperfection in small steps by intentionally leaving one piece of the task imperfect or undone. Another strategy is to set a timer for the amount of time that we're willing to dedicate to a task, and then, when the timer goes off, we stop. This prevents endless checking, fixing, and redoing. I know I am guilty of rewriting e-mails and reloading the dishwasher, neither of which is really a priority or good use of my time.

What tasks eat up your time unnecessarily due to checking, fixing, and redoing?

_____

_____

_____

Are there tasks or projects that you can apply "done is better than perfect" to? If you're not sure, ask yourself, *Is it more important for this to be done or for it to be done perfectly?*

_____

_____

_____

What do you think would happen if you left things imperfect?

_____

_____

_____

Minimize Distractions

Distractions are everywhere, especially when you have a challenging task at hand! Set yourself up for success by making it as easy as possible to do the desired task and as hard as possible to engage in other activities. The first step is to notice what distracts you and then create a plan to avoid or minimize the distraction. For example, the Internet and e-mail are huge distractions for me when I write. To deal with this, I put my phone in a drawer in another room so it takes a lot more effort to play games and check social media than if it were sitting right next to me. My kids are also a huge distraction, so sometimes I have to get out of the house and go to the library or my office so I can concentrate.

What are your biggest distractions?

_____

_____

_____

_____

When are you most likely to fall prey to these distractions?

_____

_____

_____

_____

How can you make it hard to engage in these distracting activities?

_____

_____

_____

_____

_____

Treat Yourself with Compassion

Being kind to yourself can also help you get things done. As we discussed in the last chapter, this idea can be counterintuitive, because we're used to thinking that cracking the whip and being punitive is the way to get things done. In reality, self-criticism tends to discourage people rather than motivate them. If we're hard on ourselves every time we procrastinate, we'll perpetuate avoidance and a negative self-image.

When we procrastinate, we often label ourselves "lazy," "irresponsible," or "disorganized" (or other people call us these names). These types of negative labels become part of how we see ourselves—our identity. These distorted beliefs, along with the negativity bias, mean that we'll seek out evidence to confirm that we're lazy. For example, if you take a nap, you're likely to see it as proof of laziness rather than a normal and healthy response to having been up late the night before.

In this exercise, practice noticing your critical self-talk and the names you call yourself when you procrastinate and then writing a compassionate response to try instead. Use the chart below to record some examples that have come up recently.

Event	Criticism or label	Compassionate response
I procrastinated mowing the lawn, and now it's too dark to do it.	*I'm lazy and worthless.*	*Procrastination doesn't make me lazy or worthless. I worked hard at work today, and I guess I really needed a break. It's more realistic to plan to do it first thing on Saturday.*

If you find this process helpful, you can try it with other critical self-talk statements using the worksheet called "Compassionate Responses to My Critical Self-Talk" available for download at http://www.newharbinger.com/41535.

Summary

In this chapter, we explored how overwhelm, perfectionist thinking, and fear can contribute to procrastination, and how we may miss out on opportunities, waste time, and increase stress, overwhelm, and self-criticism when we procrastinate. The exercises in this chapter targeted ways to challenge perfectionist thinking, decrease overwhelm, increase motivation, and use self-compassion to ward off procrastination. In the next chapter, we're going to look at productivity from a different standpoint and consider how doing things with greater intention and mindfulness can bring greater satisfaction and balance to our lives.

Chapter 7

From Busy to Mindfully Present

The relentless pursuit of perfection can lead to a jam-packed schedule and long hours of work. In the extreme, this can cause some problems for us. Part of our journey away from perfectionism is learning to slow down, mindfully choose our goals and commitments, and create a more balanced life.

For many of us, being constantly busy and productive is how we feel needed and valued. Busyness has become a status symbol, a measure of our worth. It's hard to fight against our core belief of being inadequate and the more-is-better mentality that pervades our culture and tells us we should be helping more, working more, earning more, buying more, exercising more, reading more, traveling more—doing more of everything and doing it effortlessly. Unfortunately, we often end up exhausted, frustrated, and unfulfilled, because in reality, no one can do it all. In this chapter and the next, we're going to look at ways to give ourselves permission to do less, ask for help, delegate, and set boundaries. We want to use our time and energy on what matters most to us, so we're going to start by getting an accurate picture of how you spend your time and whether your schedule matches your goals and values. We will then incorporate a mindfulness approach, which will help you identify your priorities and be fully present in your own life, rather than distracted and distant.

Are You Too Busy?

To get a better idea of what being overly busy and scheduled looks like, let's look at Victor's life, and then we'll do an exercise to identify how you're spending your time and determine whether you're too busy.

Victor's Story

Victor, a thirty-four-year-old accountant, is married and the father of two. He commutes thirty-five miles each way to his job at a large, highly regarded accounting firm. He uses his commute time to make phone calls and listen to the financial news. Victor likes to be the first one to the office, usually arriving by seven. Victor has proven himself to be an invaluable employee, and his boss has assigned him to several large accounts. He's often got meetings scheduled back-to-back all day, leaving him no time for lunch unless he's got a business lunch or catered meeting at midday. He powers through with the help of energy drinks and vending machine candy bars. Victor is often the last to leave the office. He says that he's trying to avoid the worst of the commuter traffic, but he often still has work to finish and dozens of e-mails to reply to. When he arrives home, usually around eight, his kids are heading to bed. He tucks them in, grabs some dinner, watches an hour of television with his wife, and then turns his laptop back on and works until he falls asleep—often on the couch.

As you can see, Victor's got a full schedule. One might say he's a workaholic—multitasking on his way to work and putting in long hours at the office, only to come home and work some more. He's too busy to eat lunch and relies on caffeine and sugar to get him through the day. Victor's busyness is probably harming his health, due to his poor eating habits and lack of sleep and exercise. He also has virtually no time for his family, friends, or hobbies.

Although what constitutes being "too" busy is subjective, there are some telltale signs that you're stretching yourself thin. Completing the checklist below will give you a sense of how many signs of excess busyness you have. As you work out what's right for you, you may also want to consider your personality traits (such as whether you're more introverted or extroverted), your energy level, your health, and your lifestyle as these can impact how drained you feel by certain activities.

Signs you might be too busy:

- ☐   You're always tired or routinely get less than seven hours of sleep.

- ☐   You regularly multitask so you can get more done.

- ☐   Your to-do list is never done.

☐ If you're raising children, they are involved in two or more activities (sports, dance, music, and so forth).

☐ You feel overwhelmed, stressed, or anxious about how much you have to do.

☐ You rely on caffeine or other stimulants to get through the day.

☐ You have a complex system of calendars, lists, reminders, and charts in order to keep track of all you have to do.

☐ Your calendar is full and sometimes double booked.

☐ You feel rushed.

☐ You feel tense or on edge.

☐ You skip meals, eat while doing other things, or eat on the go because you don't have time to prepare meals and sit down and enjoy your food.

☐ You don't have time for basic self-care activities such as going to the dentist or getting a haircut.

☐ You work on multiple goals or projects at the same time.

☐ You work nights and weekends.

☐ You feel uncomfortable when you have unscheduled time or nothing to do.

☐ You have a hard time saying no.

While there's no standardized scoring for this busyness checklist, the more items you checked, the busier your lifestyle tends to be. So, if you checked more than half of the items, this is a good opportunity to pause and take a look at the costs of being so busy and whether slowing down would offer greater relief and satisfaction.

How many items did you check off? _____ out of sixteen.

By completing the busyness checklist, did you gain any insights or notice anything new?

_____

_____

_____

_____

If busyness seems like a problem for you, the next step is to figure out exactly how you're spending your time. This will help you see the discrepancies between how you *are* spending your time and how you *want* to be spending your time, and then you can make strategic changes toward a schedule filled with meaningful activities at a pace that feels right for you.

How Are You Spending Your Time?

To get a more accurate picture of how you're spending your time, I suggest doing a time audit, a systematic way of tracking the time, duration, and type of activities throughout your day. It does take a bit of time to complete, which can be tough if you're schedule is already full, but I think you'll find it an invaluable tool for figuring out if you're spending your time on what matters most to you, especially if you checked off many of the signs of busyness in the last section. I recommend doing the time audit for at least a week, because most of us have a different schedule every day of the week. Once you've completed it, you'll calculate the amount of time you devoted to each type of activity to get a picture of how you've been spending your time—and whether that's as you want it to be. Here are the types of activities you should record as part of your time audit:

- time spent at work

- time spent driving or commuting

- family or household responsibilities

- time spent taking care of your social life or relationships

- your self-care

- the amount of time you sleep

- the time you devote to recreation or hobbies

- other obligations or commitments

For additional copies of this worksheet, called "Time Audit," visit http://www.newharbinger .com/41535.

Time Audit

Date: _____

Start time–end time	Activity	Activity type	Duration (round to nearest quarter hour)

Total Time by Activity Type

	Sun	Mon	Tues	Wed	Thurs	Fri	Sat	Total time
Work								
Driving or commuting								
Family or household responsibilities								
Social relationships								
Self-care								
Sleep								
Recreation or hobbies								
Other obligations or commitments								
Total time								

Once you have your data for the week, consider the questions below.

Which three categories consumed the majority of your time over the past week?

_____

_____

_____

Are these the categories you want to take up your time? If not, why not?

_____

_____

_____

_____

Were any categories neglected or had very low totals? Are those categories important to you?

_____

_____

_____

_____

What else stood out on your time audit?

_____

_____

_____

_____

How do you feel about the results? Were they surprising?

_____

_____

_____

The Cost of Busyness

Being busy all the time can negatively impact our relationships and health and can lead to developing resentments, making mistakes, and not achieving our goals. It's easy to take on work, commitments, volunteer projects, and even hobbies that keep us busy but don't align with our priorities. Sometimes these were initially good uses of our time, but no longer suit our needs or priorities, and other times, we may have accepted invitations or signed up for things when we knew we didn't have the time or inclination to do them.

The cost of busyness is especially high when our actions don't match with our values—the core beliefs and guiding principles that you aim to follow. Your values are the beliefs that you hold strongly and that provide a foundation for your decisions and how you choose to live your life. When our actions align with our values, we're living authentically, and we feel whole and grounded. In contrast, when our actions are out of sync with our values, we tend to feel disconnected and uncertain. This was the case for Victor. When he completed his time audit, he was shocked to see that he spent at least ninety hours per week working and commuting to work and only ten hours a week doing meaningful activities with his family. Victor valued quality family time and loving relationships, but he wasn't prioritizing those in his life. As a result, he was perpetually unfulfilled and looking to his career to satisfy him.

Might the same mismatch be at work in your life, thanks to your perfectionism? Now that you've completed your time audit, let's determine your values, so we can compare how you're spending your time with what matters most to you.

Clarifying Your Values

Values can include our spiritual or religious beliefs, morals, personal and cultural values, and political views. Some people have a clear sense of their values. And, as we've been discussing, others have lost sight of their values over time or have gone through a period of questioning and uncertainty about what they believe and what matters to them. Some haven't really had the chance to consider what their values are. Whatever your situation, the following questions will help to clarify your values.

Start to identify your values by brainstorming for five to ten minutes about values that might reflect who you are.

_____

_____

_____

_____

_____

_____

_____

_____

What makes you happiest?

_____

_____

_____

_____

_____

What do you stand for? What are you willing to speak up for or against?

_____

_____

_____

_____

_____

What values were you taught as a child? Note which you believe in and which you've rejected.

_____

_____

_____

_____

_____

Which personal traits do you value in yourself and your mentors or heroes?

_____

_____

_____

_____

_____

Which traits or values do you hope to instill in your children or grandchildren?

_____

_____

_____

_____

_____

What couldn't you live without?

_____

_____

_____

_____

_____

What do you believe?

_____

_____

_____

_____

_____

Now, write down five to ten of your most important values.

_____

_____

_____

_____

_____

_____

_____

_____

Using your values, write a short personal mission statement that describes your purpose in life and how you'd like to live.

_____

_____

_____

_____

_____

Do Your Values and Actions Align?

The final piece to this equation is to determine whether your values and actions align. Are you spending your time, energy, and money on what matters most to you, or is your schedule full of misaligned activities that make you busy but don't fulfill you? We can find out by comparing your time audit and your values.

What goals, values, or activities are most important to you? How much time do you currently spend on these pursuits?

_____

_____

_____

_____

_____

If your life was well aligned with your priorities, what would it look like? How would it be different than it is today?

_____

_____

_____

_____

_____

What changes would help you better sync your values and your activities?

_____

_____

_____

_____

_____

Keep in mind that some people may find great fulfillment with a few small tweaks to their schedule, while others need to completely overhaul their schedules in order to align their actions and values. Whatever the level of change you're contemplating, it can be made by breaking the change down into small, manageable pieces.

Creating Balance

At this point, you may have identified some things that are keeping you busy but aren't giving you fulfillment. Making changes to your schedule and commitments can be hard, especially if you like routine and predictability. But you don't have to immediately resign from every committee you're on or start running marathons. You can start small and gradually work your way toward long-term goals that reflect your priorities and values. I find that making small, incremental changes are the most realistic. They also create less anxiety.

You can work toward creating more balance in your life fifteen minutes at a time. Let's use Victor as an example again. In addition to hard work, his values included family time and health. He was putting very little time and effort into the latter two, and he realized he needed to make some changes. I encouraged Victor to spend just fifteen minutes more per day with his family and fifteen minutes doing something toward increasing his health. He chose to spend fifteen minutes in the morning packing a healthy lunch and to come home from work fifteen minutes earlier to read bedtime stories to his kids. Victor was still a long way from what most would consider a balanced life, but these were manageable changes that he could make now and continue to build on.

Using your values as a guide, what would you like to spend fifteen more minutes doing today?

_____

_____

_____

_____

_____

_____

What are you willing to spend fifteen minutes less on in order to make this time?

_____

_____

_____

_____

_____

In addition to choosing to spend our resources in ways that reflect our values, we also feel greater enjoyment when we're fully engaged in our activities. The secret to that is mindfulness.

What Is Mindfulness?

Mindfulness means being focused on the present and tuning in to all aspects of ourselves, our surroundings, and our experiences. It's focusing on the here and now, rather than being preoccupied with the past or present. Sometimes, as perfectionists, we get so wrapped up in the daily grind, or regrets or worries about how well we're doing and whether it's good enough, that we're not fully present in our own lives. When we're mindful, we're aware of what we're doing, thinking, and feeling; we're not judging or criticizing ourselves, we're just "being."

We can use mindfulness principles to gain a greater appreciation for and enjoyment of all aspects of our life. For example, when we eat mindfully, we smell the vanilla-scented aroma of a freshly baked cookie, see the crispy edges and gooey chocolate chips, taste the sweetness, and feel our teeth sink into the soft center. By contrast, when we eat mindlessly, we can easily eat several cookies without appreciating them or even realizing how many we've eaten. For most of us, mindfulness requires slowing down so we can appreciate what's right in front of us. Chronic stress and busyness make it hard to be mindful. Most of us do a lot of things on autopilot—we do them because we've always done them, without giving a lot of thought to how or what we're doing. Perhaps you mindlessly accept every invitation and request for help before thinking through whether these are activities that you have the time and inclination to do. Mindfulness helps us to pause before making a decision or taking action, so we can make choices that align with our values and bring us the most satisfaction.

Now that we've discussed mindfulness in general, we'll look at ways you can add mindfulness to your everyday life and reap the benefits of more intentional decisions, a slower pace, and fuller enjoyment of your experiences.

Adding Mindfulness to Your Life

Adding mindfulness to our lives starts with an intention. You can begin by choosing a discrete activity to practice mindfulness. Aim for something that takes five to ten minutes. You can choose something like taking a shower, driving to work, or listening to your spouse.

I intend to _____ mindfully today.

The goal is to give this activity your full attention. You may find it helpful to take a few slow, deep breaths to calm yourself before and during the activity. Your mind will inevitably drift. This is normal. When you notice your thoughts are elsewhere, simply bring your attention back to the activity you are doing. After your mindfulness practice, you can note what you experienced.

Activity

Sample response: *Walking to the coffee shop.*

Tips for being mindful in your everyday activities

♦   Do one thing at a time.

♦   Use your five senses to fully appreciate all aspects of the present.

♦   Notice how your body feels.

♦   If your thoughts wander, refocus on the present.

What was your sensory experience (sight, sound, smell, taste, touch)?

Sample response: *There were gray clouds. The wind was cold. It was loud—lots of cars and people on the street. One woman smiled at me. Most people didn't make eye contact.*

_____

_____

_____

_____

How did your body feel?

Sample response: *I was clenching my fists and felt tense from the cold.*

_____

_____

What were you thinking about during this activity? Did these thoughts distract you or were you able to stay focused on your surroundings and the activity you were doing?

Sample response: *Why didn't I bring my coat? Tara seemed angry when I told her I needed to get out. I don't think she likes me. I need to buy my mom a birthday card.*

_____

_____

_____

_____

Try adding more and more intentional mindfulness to your daily activities. I think you'll notice greater appreciation for the little things in life when you do. Some things are harder to do mindfully than others; don't be discouraged if your mind wanders and you find it tough to stay focused in the present. We refer to it as a "mindfulness *practice*" because it's something we work at. It doesn't need to be done perfectly; and there is a benefit to adding even a modest amount of imperfect mindfulness to your life.

Noticing Your Feelings

We can also use mindfulness to tune in to our feelings. We perfectionists tend to be so busy and distracted or so goal-focused that we don't even notice our feelings. And other times, our feelings are uncomfortable, like the ones about our shortcomings, mistakes, and inadequacies, that we push them away so we don't have to feel them. But feelings provide valuable information, and we ultimately benefit from learning to tune in and listen to them. For example, when Victor started to pay attention to his feelings, he noticed he was feeling resentful and exhausted. He was tempted to just shrug it off and assume he was overreacting—his first thought was, *It's nothing*. But Victor knew that, instead, he could validate his feelings and be curious about them. He's feeling angry and exhausted for a reason. By asking himself some questions, he knew that he could get a better sense of what these feelings were trying to tell him so that he could act accordingly. In this case, Victor took that path, and his curiosity about his feelings helped him realize that he feels resentful of his colleagues who seem to do far less work yet get the same bonuses and accolades. And he's exhausted by the long hours and stressful work situation. Victor can now use this information to help him find solutions that will help him feel less angry and more rested.

To bring your feelings into greater awareness, you can practice checking in with yourself several times a day. I recommend doing it morning, noon, and night. Pairing the check-in with mealtime or bedtime makes it easier to remember, but you can choose whatever times work well for you. Just try to keep them consistent and spread out over the course of the day. During each check-in, identify your feelings, notice where you experience the emotions in your body (many people find it easier to notice physical manifestations of their feelings), explore why you're feeling this way, and practice acceptance. The purpose of this exercise is to increase awareness of feelings, not to try to change them. There is a list of feeling words at the end of the book (appendix C) that can help you identify a wide range of feelings.

Date	Feelings	Where do you feel the emotion in your body?	Why might you feel this way?	Accept your feelings
April 12	Worried	Stomachache, rapid heartbeat	I'm giving an important presentation at work tomorrow.	It's normal to feel worried about presenting in front of a big group. Lots of successful movie stars get stage fright. It doesn't mean anything's wrong with me.

Mindful Decision Making

Perfectionist thinking can make decision making hard, because we feel like we need to make the "right" decision all the time and don't allow any room for errors. We get caught up in obsessive thoughts about all the things that can go wrong or ways we've messed up in the past. These types of negative ruminations make it challenging to see all our options and evaluate them realistically. Mindfulness can help us focus on the decision at hand with less worry about what's happened in the past or what might happen in the future.

In this chapter, we're focusing on the decisions we make regarding how to spend our time and, ultimately, what matters enough to make it onto our calendars. We don't have to keep choosing busyness because it's what we've always done, and we can consciously consider all our options without overthinking them. Mindfulness also helps to keep things in perspective, so we don't exaggerate the repercussions of a "bad" decision, for example. You can use the questions that follow to help you mindfully consider whether to add something to your calendar or to-do list.

Think of an activity, goal, or commitment you have planned. How do you feel about it?

_____

_____

_____

_____

_____

Is this activity, goal, or commitment in line with your values?

_____

_____

_____

_____

Whose goal is this? Is it important to you, or are you seeking recognition or trying to avoid disappointing someone?

_____

_____

_____

_____

Will this activity bring you joy?

_____

_____

_____

Are you responsible for doing this task? If yes, do you need to do it all yourself?

_____

_____

_____

Can you ask for help or delegate some of it? If so, to whom?

_____

_____

_____

_____

For a "Mindful Decision Making" worksheet you can use to consider these questions for other activities in your life, visit http://www.newharbinger.com/41535.

One Thing at a Time

Another way to slow down and be more mindful is to do one thing at a time. For those of us with high standards, big goals, and long to-do lists, multitasking seems like a godsend.

When do you multitask? What activities do you do at the same time?

_____

_____

_____

Unfortunately, multitasking's not all it's cracked up to be. It doesn't actually help us get more done. Our brains can only focus on one thing at a time, so when we multitask and try to make our brains do to a number of things at once, the quality of our attention and work declines. Multitasking gives us the illusion of efficiency, but in reality, we sometimes have to redo tasks, or we get them done more slowly, because our attention is pulled in multiple directions. As we've discussed, mindfulness is the opposite of multitasking. Although it can seem slower, mindfulness helps us to work more thoroughly, purposefully, and happily.

Even if you accept that multitasking isn't efficient, it can be hard to break the habit. We have essentially trained our brains to desire a high level of stimulation, so it feels strange and uncomfortable to do just one thing at a time. But trying to do one thing at a time is another way for us to slow down, thoughtfully choose what we're doing, and be more mindfully present.

Your goal doesn't need to be to completely eliminate multitasking—that's probably not realistic. Instead, the goal is to choose mindfully when you're multitasking and when you're being fully present. Again, these decisions will line up with your values. For example, if you're trying to connect with your family, you might refrain from using cell phones during dinner and on family outings, but you might continue to listen to podcasts while running on the treadmill.

Let's try "unitasking"—working on just one thing at a time. We're going to again practice this change in fifteen-minute intervals to allow you to get used to it gradually. Even this short amount of time can make many people feel restless. Try to tolerate the discomfort for as long as you can, but it's okay to start with five or ten minutes and work your way up, if needed.

Choose one activity to do without multitasking. Set a timer for fifteen minutes, and do only that activity—nothing else.

How did it feel to do one thing at a time?

_____

_____

_____

What were you thinking?

_____

_____

_____

Did you notice anything new or different?

_____

_____

_____

Did you experience greater focus or enjoyment?

_____

_____

_____

It's okay if your answer to the last question was no. Increased focus and enjoyment may not come right away. You may need to practice unitasking quite a few times before your nervous system calms down and you find it feels good.

Gratitude

Gratitude is a simple but powerful mindfulness practice. It works by shifting our focus to what's good, beautiful, hopeful, and positive right at this moment. Gratitude helps us to appreciate the small things in life that are easy to take for granted, like fresh, hot coffee in the morning or your children laughing. Research has shown that gratitude contributes to better physical health, mental health, self-esteem, and stronger connections to others (Emmons and McCullough 2003). We can also use gratitude to look inward and acknowledge our internal strengths and resources—things that, as perfectionists, we often discount. Perfectionists can also benefit from gratitude because it draws our busy minds to the present and away from the worries, fears, self-doubt, and self-criticism that so often plague us.

To begin a gratitude practice, I suggest writing down three to five things you're grateful for several times per week. You can start in the space provided and then you may want to continue with a journal or notepad left at your bedside (or the worksheet, called "Gratitude Journal," that's available at http://www.newharbinger.com/41535).

Date	I am grateful for...

A fun alternative to a gratitude journal is to make a gratitude jar or box. Find an empty container. If you're so inclined, you can make it look pretty by decorating it with craft supplies. Several times a week, write three to five things you're grateful for on small slips of paper and put them into the gratitude jar. Any time you're feeling discouraged or unmotivated, you can take a few of your gratitude slips from the jar and reread them to get a little happiness boost.

Gratitude has even more power when it's expressed; both the giver and receiver feel the positive effects (Seligman et al. 2005). Gratitude sets a positive tone for a family or workplace. So if you express gratitude, those around you are more likely to do so too.

Whom in your life might you wish to express gratitude to? If you're interested in taking your gratitude practice further, use the chart below to plan out whom you'll express gratitude to and for what. Try writing and mailing a thank-you note to the people you list, or simply express your feelings verbally.

Date	Whom will you express gratitude to today?	For?

For a more challenging gratitude practice, try being grateful for your imperfections!

How have your mistakes and imperfections helped you learn, grow, and become who you are today?

_____

_____

_____

_____

Does answering this question change how you feel about those mistakes and imperfections?

_____

_____

_____

_____

Summary

In this chapter, I asked you to consider whether you're "too busy" doing things that don't align with your values and priorities to prove your worth. Mindfulness, in the form of using all our senses, noticing our feelings, mindful decision making, and doing one thing at a time, can help us to slow down and be more intentional in how we spend our time. When we practice letting go of commitments and activities that don't contribute to our goals or happiness, we find greater contentment and balance. Gratitude is a practice that helps us move away from self-doubt and self-criticism and focus on our strengths and the things that bring us joy, ultimately helping us to be physically and emotionally healthier.

It's not easy to stop doing things we've always done or to say no to people who are counting on us, even when we know these activities aren't serving our own needs. In the next chapter, we will work on ways to ask for what we need and set boundaries without feeling bad, even when other people are displeased or disappointed.

Chapter 8

From People-Pleasing to Being Assertive

People-pleasing is another aspect of perfectionism that can cause stress, diminish our self-worth, and squash our authentic selves. Our all-or-nothing thinking tells us that disappointing people means we aren't perfect; we're failures or inadequate. Wanting to please everyone all the time is another unrealistic expectation that perfectionists have for themselves. We want so much to be validated by others and to avoid conflicts, but it's impossible to always please others no matter how good we are and how hard we try. In this chapter, we will discuss not only how people-pleasing is an unrealistic expectation but also why trying to be perfect in other people's eyes isn't always good for us and how assertive communication skills can help us be more authentic.

What Is People-Pleasing?

People-pleasing is a compelling need to do things to make other people happy, have them like us, or to avoid conflict, even when doing so causes us problems. Because perfectionists doubt their worth and abilities, they seek validation by trying to do the right thing, say the right thing, looking perfect, and meeting others' expectations. Lorenzo and Kate illustrate two different ways that people-pleasing can manifest.

Lorenzo's Story

Lorenzo tries to keep everyone in his life happy. He grew up in a family that believed children should be seen and not heard. He didn't imagine that at forty-three years old, he'd still be afraid to stand up to his opinionated father, but he is. Lorenzo works for his father in their family business, which is a constant source of frustration. Lorenzo has his own ideas about how to run the business, but he's not empowered to share his ideas or implement them. He feels guilty, but he's counting the days until his father retires so he can do things his own way. Lorenzo is also a loving husband and father. He dotes on his children, indulging them in new video games and sneakers, while he rarely spends money on himself. At home, Lorenzo defers to his wife's opinion. "Whatever you want, Honey" is his default answer to everything. He thinks this response is a loving gesture, but it irritates his wife. "Don't you have an opinion about anything!" she complains. But Lorenzo doesn't want to argue. He just wants everyone to get along and be happy.

Kate's Story

Kate is very sensitive to what people think of her. When a stranger in the coffee shop rolled his eyes at Kate's order, she couldn't shake the feeling that she'd done something wrong. The day before, her face had burned with embarrassment when she held up the checkout line at the grocery store while the bagger went back to get her a new carton of eggs. *Why didn't I check to make sure they weren't cracked?* she scolded herself. She was sure the cashier, bagger, and everyone in line behind her thought she was the biggest idiot of all time. Over the years, Kate has found herself teaching summer school, leading a girl scout troop, fostering kittens, and house-sitting for neighbors, all of which were kind and generous, but things she detests. She didn't want to let anyone down.

People-pleasers like Lorenzo and Kate derive some of their identity and self-worth from doing things for others. It feels good to be a dependable, go-to person who can fix things and make people feel better, but it also causes problems for us.

Isn't Making People Happy a Good Thing?

Most of us were taught to be agreeable and charitable and to care about other people's feelings and help them out in times of need. These are wonderful qualities. The problem is that when our self-worth is dependent on making people happy, we will repeatedly compromise our own needs to please others, and we often care more about other people's opinions and values than our own.

Perfectionists are prime candidates for people-pleasing because we seek external validation to prove our worth. We tend to have doubts and insecurities that we're trying to overcome by achieving more, being the best, looking impeccable, or doing the right thing. Our quest for perfection is largely a quest to please others, because when others give us a stamp of approval, we feel like we belong, like we've earned our place at the table.

Part of being and looking perfect is meeting other people's expectations. Essentially, if others are disappointed or displeased with us, we haven't achieved our goal of perfection. We aren't good enough.

Our fears of failure, inadequacy, conflict, and rejection can keep us stuck and reluctant to take chances and do new things. People-pleasing is another way that we try to manage these fears. We think that if we do everything that's expected of us, it will guarantee that others like us, need us, and will stick around. We don't really have any control over whether people reject or criticize us, but being agreeable all the time gives us a much-desired sense of control and the illusion that we will avoid disapproval and conflict. Let's reflect on what people-pleasing looks like in your life and whether it's working well for you.

In what ways or situations do you silence your own opinions, ideas, wants, or needs?

_____

_____

_____

What are the benefits of keeping your thoughts and opinions to yourself?

☐ You avoid conflict.

☐ You avoid rejection.

☐ You avoid embarrassment, guilt, or shame.

☐ People like you.

☐ People count on you.

☐ You feel good about helping.

☐ _____

☐ _____

☐ _____

As you reflect on the list of the benefits of people-pleasing, you probably noticed that people-pleasing allows you to "play it safe" or avoid anxiety provoking situations and feelings. People are less likely to criticize you when you always agree with them or don't put forth any original ideas or work. On the other hand, there are some down sides to people-pleasing as well.

What are the drawbacks of keeping your thoughts, ideas, and opinions to yourself?

- ☐ You're overcommitted and tired, because you don't say no.

- ☐ You feel guilty when you do say no or disagree.

- ☐ You're resentful when you take on things you don't want to.

- ☐ You feel stressed.

- ☐ You don't value yourself.

- ☐ People don't respect you when you're passive and don't have your own opinions.

- ☐ Family and friends get frustrated when you don't have opinions and ideas.

- ☐ People don't really know you deeply.

- ☐ You miss out on opportunities or continue to do things you don't like.

- ☐ You do things that go against your values (or fail to stand up for your values).

- ☐ You're inconvenienced or financially strained as a result of putting other people's needs first.

- ☐ You feel like you can't please everyone, no matter how hard you try.

- ☐ You feel like you're missing out on your own life.

- ☐ You don't ask for what you want or need.

- ☐ You've lost track of who you are, what you want, and what's important to you.

- ☐ Other: _____

- ☐ _____

- ☐ _____

How do you think your life would be improved if you could be more authentic and assertive?

_____

_____

_____

_____

People-pleasing tends to put all the importance on what other people want and diminishes our own opinions and needs. As we've done with other perfectionist traits, we want to moderate our desire to please others so that it includes taking care of and staying true to ourselves. It's possible to be both assertive and kind and to consider our own needs as well as those of others.

Learning to Be Assertive

People often confuse being assertive with being aggressive. They imagine being assertive as being harsh, demanding, and self-serving. Naturally, that's a turnoff, but it's actually more aggressive than assertive.

There are three basic styles of communication: passive, aggressive, and assertive. Passive communication is the form most associated with people-pleasing. When we're passive, we fail to respond or speak up; we let others take the lead. For example, Lorenzo was passive with his father and didn't share his ideas or ask to make the changes he wanted in the business.

Aggressive communication doesn't take other people into account. It essentially says, "My opinions and needs are more important than yours, and I don't care if I hurt or disrespect you in order to get what I want." Aggressive communication includes behaviors such as yelling, rude gestures, threatening, intimidating, and imposing on someone's personal space (standing too close).

Assertiveness is the middle ground between passive and aggressive. It's direct, calm, and respectful. It allows us to directly express our feelings in ways that don't hurt or violate those of others. Assertive communication increases the chances that our needs will be met. It also contributes to healthy, happy relationships, because it's respectful.

Assertive communication is the gold standard—the way we all aspire to express ourselves. In the next section, we'll practice specific assertive communication skills.

What Stands in Your Way of Being Assertive

Take a few minutes to identify the barriers you face in implementing assertive communication, so we'll know how to overcome them.

☐ **Lack of practice:** Effective communication is a set of skills, and if you never learned assertive communication skills or had them modeled for you, you can't possibly know how to use them. Or you may have learned or read about the basics of effective communication, but you haven't had much practice. It's always easier to do what we've always done rather than try something that we're not yet skilled in.

☐ **Not feeling worthy:** When you believe your opinions, needs, or wants aren't important, it's hard to feel motivated to stand up for them.

☐ **Fear of hurting people's feelings:** If you pride yourself on being a "nice" person, you may shy away from assertive communication because you're afraid of offending or hurting someone's feelings.

☐ **Wanting to keep the peace:** Conflict is scary for a lot of us. Expressing yourself might lead to a disagreement or an argument. It's true that there's a risk that others will disagree with you or might be downright mean and hurtful. But the fear of that hostility (or even actual hostility) is no reason to continue to bury your own needs (later in this chapter, you'll read more about letting go of other people's reactions and expectations).

☐ **Fear of rejection:** Rejection comes in many forms. Sometimes the threat of rejection is stated outright ("I'm going to divorce you") and sometimes it's our internal fears and insecurities based on cognitive distortions or past events. In either case, a fear that someone will be so displeased with us that they'll leave is a powerful force in keeping us silent.

☐ **Guilt:** You feel like it's wrong to say no or ask for what you need, and when you do, you feel extremely guilty.

Practicing Assertive Communication Skills

Learning new skills always takes a significant amount of practice before we feel comfortable and confident with them. Below are some of the basic skills for assertive communication. Try to practice using them daily. To get started, practice them in safe, less conflictual situations and work your way up to using them with more difficult people and issues.

The basic tenet of assertive communication is to express yourself clearly, calmly, and respectfully. It's tempting to expect that others will know what we want or need without us having to ask. Unfortunately, that's a fantasy! We must speak up in a respectful way and share what's going on with us, which, of course, can be scary when our perfectionist thinking shows up.

What Do You Want?

In order to communicate effectively, we have to first know what we want to communicate. Sometimes our feelings aren't immediately obvious to us. In which case, we need to first pause and figure out what it is we want to say. As we did in the Noticing Your Feelings exercise in chapter 7, we can turn our attention inward and check in with ourselves to bring greater awareness to our internal state. You can start with these simple questions.

How do I feel right now?

_____

_____

What do I need?

_____

_____

Getting Your Message Across

"I statements" are one of the simplest and most effective tools you can put in your assertive communication toolkit. Beginning a sentence with "you" tends to feel blaming and accusatory, which often leads to a defensive response. An "I statement" avoids this by using a basic formula:

"I feel _____ when _____.

And I'd like _____."

Notice the difference in the statements below.

- You statement: *You're so inconsiderate. You're late and didn't bother to text me.*

- I statement: *I feel frustrated when you come home late without letting me know. I'd like you to text me when you're running late.*

Let's practice with a couple of examples.

Maria's neighbor had a loud party again last night—the second time this week. Maria has to get up at five in the morning to go to work. She's tired and frustrated at her neighbor's disregard.

You statement: _____

I statement: _____

Charlotte's client hired her for eight hours of videography services. The contract clearly stated that she charges 150 percent of her standard rate beyond eight hours. On the day of the event, the client asked her to stay for two additional hours. Now the client refuses to pay Charlotte for the overtime.

You statement: _____

I statement: _____

John's mother calls him every day. She loves to tell him about all the happenings in her small town—her neighbor planted peonies yesterday, her cat caught a mouse in the garage, a new Starbucks is going in on the corner. John's really not interested in most of it and feels stressed out with his own busy schedule. He doesn't know how to get his mom off the phone.

You statement: _____

I statement: _____

In addition to using I statements, we should avoid generalizations such as always and never, because they can trigger defensiveness, escalate tension, and shut down open communication. They're also rarely accurate. Notice how these statements feel with and without generalizations.

- "You always leave your dishes in the sink! Can you please put them in the dishwasher?"

- "I noticed you left your dishes in the sink. Can you please put them in the dishwasher?"

This simple change can increase the likelihood that your message will be well received.

Assertive communication is also direct. Using a lot of qualifiers or excuses can discount our message and undermine our confidence. Compare the difference between these two statements:

- "I'm really sorry. I missed what you said. Sometimes I'm really slow. Can you repeat that?"

- "Can you repeat that?"

The explanations in the first example detract from your request and imply that there's something wrong with you or you're asking something unreasonable.

Let's further practice differentiating passive, aggressive, and assertive communication with the following exercise. Imagine your significant other asked you what you'd like for dinner. Identify what you want and then practice writing a passive, aggressive, and assertive response. Here's a sample response to help you get started.

I want: *I want something healthy, like a salad.*

Passive: *I don't care; whatever you want is fine.*

Aggressive: *I already told you I'm eating healthy. Why are you always suggesting pizza or burgers? You're so inconsiderate!*

Assertive: *I'm trying to eat healthfully, so a salad would be great. I'd really appreciate it if you'd pick up some spinach on your way home.*

Try this exercise on your own: imagine that your boss has given you another huge project when you're already overworked.

I want: _____

Passive: _____

Aggressive: _____

_____

Assertive: _____

_____

Practicing these strategies will help you find assertive ways to communicate at work and at home. As I said, it takes practice, and it isn't easy at first. But like most things, it gets easier the more you practice.

Staying Calm, Cool, and Collected

When we're assertive, we want to express our feelings but not let them overtake us; we can deliver our message most effectively when we remain calm. So if you're feeling angry or upset, it helps to take a break, do something to intentionally calm your mind and body (such as journaling, doing twenty jumping jacks, or deep breathing), and put your thoughts together before proceeding. Otherwise, we run the risk of reverting to passivity or losing our tempers and becoming aggressive.

Identify three things that help you calm down.

- _____

- _____

- _____

Writing a script is another strategy that you can use when you're anticipating a difficult conversation or you're feeling upset or overwhelmed. Writing down what we want to say helps us clarify our main points, be direct but not accusatory, and process our feelings about the situation. I've done this myself and found it very helpful. I don't often follow the script verbatim, but taking the time to write it down has helped me deliver my point of view more effectively when I'm feeling stressed.

With a challenging situation in mind, write a script of what you want to say.

_____

_____

_____

_____

Owning Your Self-Worth

When we value ourselves and feel valued by others, it's easier to be assertive. However, as we've been discussing throughout this book, perfectionism is fueled by feelings of inadequacy—hence the need to prove and perfect ourselves. Instead of focusing on our feelings of inadequacy as a barrier to assertiveness, we can view assertiveness as a way to gain self-confidence and self-esteem. In other words, we don't have to wait until we feel completely confident and worthy to be assertive. We can stretch ourselves a little bit beyond our comfort zone, and by practicing being more assertive, we will come to feel more worthwhile.

Often our insecurities are based on things we were told as children; they're old tapes that we keep playing even though they aren't accurate or helpful. Until we take the time to investigate them, we believe these old tapes playing in our subconscious. They might sound like this: *No one cares what I think* or *I don't want to say the wrong thing* or *If I'm honest about my feelings, she might get mad.* These thoughts are likely to perpetuate our perfectionism and passivity, because they reinforce the concerns we have about what people will think of us and because they hinder our ability to value our own thoughts and feelings and share them respectfully.

Think of a situation in which it's hard for you to be assertive. Briefly describe the situation.

_____

_____

_____

_____

_____

Now notice your feelings and self-talk, particularly around whether your opinions and feelings matter or are worthy of being shared. What are you saying to yourself that may be a barrier to assertiveness?

_____

_____

_____

_____

_____

Where do you think you got the notion that your feelings and needs are less important than other people's or that you should silence yourself in order to keep the peace?

_____

_____

_____

_____

Recognizing that these beliefs originated with other people can help you separate your own beliefs from those of others. You don't have to continue to accept what other people have told you as fact. You can choose to develop your own beliefs about yourself and use them to direct your actions.

Who gets to decide if your feelings and needs matter? Do you think they matter?

_____

_____

_____

_____

How does it feel to decide that you're worthy regardless of what others say or think?

_____

_____

_____

_____

Owning your self-worth can be a powerful experience, especially if it's new for you. How you feel about yourself is something that you get to control. On the other hand, we can't control how other people will respond to our assertiveness. This is why letting go of the outcome is also an important piece of our communication skills.

Letting Go of the Outcome

Sometimes people shy away from assertive communication because they're afraid it will hurt other people's feelings or make them angry. Ironically, assertive communication will actually minimize the chances of hurting others. But no matter how skilled we are at communicating, we can't control how others respond to our words and actions. If we speak up only when we're guaranteed a positive response, we end up minimizing and repressing a lot of our feelings and needs (which, as we have seen, creates a whole host of problems). Instead, the solution is to lean into the uncertainty and let go of the outcome. We can only do our best to deliver our message respectfully.

To help with this, I like to use a supportive mantra. Reading the mantra or saying it aloud reinforces your intention to focus on what you can control, to value yourself, and not to worry or fixate on the outcome. Try using this mantra or adapt it as needed to support your goals.

I am learning to be more assertive. I'm learning that it's not my job to make everyone happy. Being assertive is a way to honor my true self and be more authentic. When I hesitate, I will remind myself that my feelings and needs matter. I deserve to express them regardless of what other people think or how they react. I can only control myself, and I am choosing to let go of the outcome.

Releasing Guilt

Guilt is a familiar feeling for perfectionists; it's the belief that you've done something wrong, and it's a common barrier to assertiveness. It works like this: Even though I'm busy, I feel like it would be selfish (wrong) to tell my neighbor that I can't babysit her son. So I don't say anything and do the babysitting, but I'm unhappy about it. Guilt prevented me from being assertive and saying, "I'm sorry, but I've got a bunch of errands to run this afternoon, and I can't help you out."

We're quick to assume that setting boundaries, taking care of ourselves, or displeasing someone is wrong—we should never do it. This leaves us guilt-ridden whenever we assert ourselves or when our needs conflict with someone else's. We tend to prioritize other peoples' needs above our own. Ultimately, it's impossible to please everyone all the time, and when we try, we end up unhappy and stressed out.

It's normal to care about what other people think. But one of the biggest people-pleasing traps is to act as if everyone's opinion matters equally. This leads us to try to please everyone rather than being selective and building up a tolerance to some people being displeased with us. We don't have to stop caring what others think; we just want to be selective. We can reduce our feelings of guilt by sorting out whose opinion really matters.

Make a list of the people whose opinions matter, whom you try to please, or whom you might stay quiet around in order to avoid conflict. They can be people you know well or strangers (in which case, you can write something like "people on the street" or "waitress"). Think of people in all areas of your life.

- _____
- _____
- _____
- _____
- _____
- _____
- _____
- _____
- _____
- _____
- _____
- _____
- _____

Rank order the people on your list according to how much their opinion really matters to you. For example, you might rank your spouse as number 1 (his or her opinion matters the most), your best friend as number 2, your mother as number 3, and so on.

Do you have a close relationship with the people highly ranked on your list? Usually, the closer the relationship, the more you value someone's opinion. However, many of us go out of our way to please even the people at the bottom of the list, and this creates unnecessary guilt.

Brené Brown, PhD, describes it like this in her book *Daring Greatly*: "I carry a small sheet of paper in my wallet that has written on it the names of people whose opinions of me matter… To be on my list, you have to be what I call a 'stretch-mark friend'—our connection has been stretched and pulled so much that it's become part of who we are, a second skin, and there are a few scars to prove it… The important thing is not to discount the stretch-mark friends to gain the approval of the strangers who are being mean and nasty or are too cool" (2012, 171).

As perfectionists, we're trying to mold ourselves into someone other people want us to be, so we'll fit in or gain their approval, but most of these people haven't earned the right to be on our list. Often, we don't even know them. But then, nevertheless, we feel guilty when we don't meet their expectations.

The other problem that we run into is holding ourselves to a higher standard than everyone else. We think it's wrong for us to do things that are perfectly okay for our friends and colleagues to do.

Let's explore the beliefs that can contribute to guilt by identifying three situations in which you prioritize other people's wants and needs and suppress your own, even when doing so causes you harm (for example, you're inconvenienced, it's a financial strain, it contributes to exhaustion or illness, it prevents you from tending to your needs, or it goes against your values). It could be getting the wrong order at a restaurant and eating it anyway because you don't want to be difficult or finishing a proposal while on vacation because your boss wanted it done.

Situation 1: _____

_____

Situation 2: _____

_____

Situation 3: _____

_____

Now imagine a friend were in the same situations. Would it be wrong for your friend to speak up or ask for what they need in these situations?

_____

_____

_____

Are you holding yourself to a different standard? Is it helpful?

_____

_____

_____

Try rewriting each situation to affirm that it's okay for you to speak up even if others don't like it. This creates the basis for self-talk that supports being more assertive. Here's an example: "It is reasonable to ask for my meal to be remade if it's not prepared as I ordered it. People do this all the time, and it's not being difficult."

Situation 1: _____

_____

Situation 2: _____

_____

Situation 3: _____

_____

Summary

On the surface, it seems like being agreeable and meeting expectations is a good thing, but as we've discussed in this chapter, bending over backward to please others isn't always in our own best interest. When we silence ourselves in order to be validated, our needs go unnoticed and unmet. Assertive communication allows us to respectfully ask for what we need and to be our imperfect selves. Practicing assertive communication can improve our relationships as well as boost our self-esteem and decrease feelings of guilt. When we don't speak our truth and have our needs acknowledged, we're likely to grow resentful and angry. In the next chapter, we'll learn to notice, accept, and release our anger.

Chapter 9

From Anger to Peace

Anger doesn't fit into most people's vision of being perfect. If we were perfect, we'd be happy all the time, do things effortlessly, and be even tempered and satisfied with ourselves and others at all times. This isn't anybody's reality. We all have a complex array of feelings, and they all serve a purpose—even anger. In this chapter, you'll gain a greater understanding of what anger is and what purpose it serves. You will practice noticing the physical signs of anger and how your perfectionist thoughts and expectations contribute to anger. And, finally, you'll learn several strategies to help you transform your anger, release perfectionism, and feel at peace.

What Is Anger and Why Does It Matter?

Anger is a normal and important feeling. Feelings aren't "good" or "bad"; they all have a purpose. So feeling angry doesn't mean you're a bad, mean, or flawed person.

Anger is sometimes thought to be bad or wrong because it's confused with aggression or violence. Anger is a feeling, and often it's letting us know that we've been hurt, wronged, or mistreated. Aggression and violence, on the other hand, are actions that may be expressions of anger, but we don't have to act in ways that hurt us or others when we're angry.

Sometimes we're angry at others because they haven't lived up to our expectations, and sometimes we're angry at ourselves for the same reason. We also might feel angry at people in our lives who expect us to be perfect. As Rachel and Vivian show in the following examples, anger can provide us with important information that something is wrong.

Rachel's Story

In addition to working four nights a week as an emergency room nurse, Rachel cooks all her family's meals, washes the dishes, does the laundry, and cleans the house. No one offers to help. Rachel feels unappreciated but doesn't ask for help. Day after day, her anger builds until one day she lashes out at her family—yelling, crying, and vowing to go on strike to teach them all a lesson. Rachel's anger was letting her know she felt unappreciated. Anger was a cue that she needed to speak up and ask for help.

Vivian's Story

Vivian's anger, on the other hand, is directed at herself. Her supervisor suggested that she apply for an exciting opportunity in the company's Paris office. Vivian had always wanted to live in Europe, and this job would also include a big promotion and raise. But Vivian didn't get the job. She's sure she came across as arrogant and overconfident in the interview and can't stop replaying the interview in her head. Her anger might be telling her she's disappointed, hurt, or feeling unworthy.

It's tempting to ignore anger. It's a difficult emotion to navigate, one that's generally not socially acceptable to express (especially for women), and it goes against our desire to be perfect. However, anger doesn't go away when we ignore it. Suppressed anger accumulates until it reaches a breaking point, and then it reveals itself, sometimes dramatically. It shows up as health problems like headaches or insomnia, we explode with yelling or physical aggression, or we behave in passive-aggressive ways, such as "forgetting" to do something. Suppressed anger can also contribute to depression and anxiety. It's important for our physical and emotional health to learn to notice and cope with anger in healthy ways.

Noticing Anger

Low levels of anger, the small annoyances and frustrations of everyday life, often go unnoticed, because we aren't tuned in to our feelings or we're trying to deny feeling angry. We often think that it's wrong to be angry and that we shouldn't be irritated by things; we should be able to let them go effortlessly. Unfortunately, "let it go" has become synonymous with "ignore it." We pretend it's not bothering us, which is precisely what we don't want to do. Truly letting go of anger is an active process and does take effort. It helps to start recognizing different amounts or types of anger.

What are some words that you use to describe being slightly angry?

_____   _____

_____   _____

_____   _____

Being moderately angry?

_____   _____

_____   _____

_____   _____

Being really, really angry?

_____   _____

_____   _____

_____   _____

High levels of anger are obvious to most people. It's the low levels that we often miss. That's why we want to tune in to that first group of words and begin to notice anger as it brews. We can think of anger as drops of water falling into a cup. Over time, small experiences of anger fill the cup, and it reaches the brim. Although it's more likely that your cup is being filled by a series of small drops over the course of days or weeks, it's also possible for one situation to fill your cup in one fell swoop. Just like a cup of water, if we never pour any of our anger out, it will eventually fill up and spill over the top. The anger spilling out often takes the form of yelling, slamming the door, and cursing, or at least mumbling under our breath, which aren't healthy or effective ways to deal with anger. Sometimes our reactions catch us off guard; we didn't realize we were this angry, because we missed the warning signs. The fuller the cup gets, the harder it becomes to empty it in a healthy way.

What are some things that fill your cup with anger?

_____

_____

_____

_____

Physical Signs of Anger

In addition to paying attention to the things that trigger our anger, we want to pay attention to our bodies and try to notice the physical sensations that tell us anger is building.

Which of these physical signs of anger do you experience?

☐ rapid heart rate   ☐ tightening in the jaw, clenching teeth

☐ butterflies in your stomach   ☐ trembling

☐ clenched fists   ☐ pacing

☐ headache   ☐ crying

☐ muscle tension   ☐ fatigue

☐ warm or hot face   ☐ insomnia

☐ sweating   ☐ isolating

Thoughts That Contribute to Anger

Our perfectionist thinking can also contribute to feeling angry and be a cue to help us notice our feelings. At the beginning of the chapter, I told you about Rachel, whose anger grew out of feeling overworked and unappreciated. Below are some of Rachel's thoughts. They are focused on the negatives and contain absolutes (nobody, only, always) and unmet expectations that fuel her anger.

• Nobody notices how much work I do.

- I'm the only one who cleans the house.

- My family is a bunch of lazy slobs.

- A good mother cooks for her family.

- The house should always be clean.

- Carl [her husband] and the kids always leave soap on the dishes.

Rachel's anger serves an important purpose in letting her know that something needs to change in the division of labor in her family, but it is hard for her to identify what she needs and to ask for it assertively when she's this angry. Noticing perfectionist thoughts that increase our anger and modifying them can help us communicate more effectively and improve our relationships with others and ourselves. Your perfectionist thoughts might include a variety of things:

- I should always have the right answer.

- I should never hurt people's feelings.

- I should always eat healthfully.

- I should excel at everything.

- I should know what to do.

- I should achieve all my goals.

- I should never make a mistake.

- I should never be late or forgetful.

- My spouse should be affectionate.

- Life should be fair.

- Children should respect their parents.

- People who work hard deserve to be successful.

These perfectionist thoughts reflect expectations that we have for ourselves or other people. It can be helpful to conceptualize anger as resulting from unmet expectations. So recognizing your expectations (especially those that are repeatedly unmet) can help you recognize your anger.

Using the list of things that fill up your cup with anger, identify your expectations and underlying assumptions.

Anger trigger	Expectation	Assumption
My wife overdrew the checking account.	I expect her to stick to our budget.	She doesn't care about our finances and is more interested in what she wants than our shared goals.

Noticing unmet expectations is also helpful because we can change our expectations. Understandably, most perfectionists don't like the idea of lowering or changing their standards. For so long, we've prided ourselves and pushed ourselves and others based on them. But many of them are unrealistic and cause us emotional pain. Choosing to lower our expectations isn't defeat or failure, it's choosing to be happier. It increases the chances that our expectations and standards will be met, and we'll experience greater satisfaction and peace and less anger and frustration. In the next exercise, you will reframe your expectations so they are more attainable.

Try to eliminate all-or-nothing thinking (words such as never, always, all, every, success, failure, good, bad) and should statements (words such as should, must, ought).

Current expectation	More realistic expectation
I expect myself to eat clean all the time.	*I expect myself to eat healthfully most of the time, but I realize my diet doesn't have to be perfect to be healthy.*

Daily Tracking

Tracking is another valuable strategy. Keeping track of something in an organized fashion brings awareness and accountability. It's especially helpful with anger, because anger often builds over hours or days. Anger, like most things, is easiest to deal with when it's an irritation rather than a full-fledged rage. Rating and tracking your anger can help you manage it proactively by noticing it and reducing it before it reaches the point of no return.

I use a simple rating scale of 0 to 10. I suggest rating your anger twice a day (morning and night). You can add a midday check-in if you find it helpful. Simply record it on the chart below, your calendar, or a note-taking app. If you're doing the Noticing Your Feelings exercise in chapter 7, you can easily incorporate anger tracking by paying particular attention to any feelings that are associated with anger (frustrated, irritated, annoyed, furious) and rating them on a ten-point scale.

Note your level of anger and what is causing it.

Date	Morning anger level (0–10) What's contributing to this level of anger?	Evening anger level (0–10) What's contributing to this level of anger?

Transforming Your Anger

While anger is useful, we don't want to stew in it or let it build. There are many ways to decrease our anger. You may need to try a variety of strategies to find what works for you and is realistic for your lifestyle. It's good to have different strategies for different circumstances. Obviously, you can't take a hot bath in the middle of the workday, but it might be great on Saturday night.

Write About It

Writing or journaling is one of my favorite therapeutic strategies, because it's quick, effective, and can be done almost anywhere. And writing is a safe way to unload your feelings. It allows you to vent about anything that's irritating you without negative consequences; no one will know what you're writing or tell you that your feelings are wrong or be hurt or offended. In addition, writing can help you process and sort through your thoughts and feelings. Writing often leads to greater clarity and new insights, which can be helpful in seeing things from a different perspective or helping you make decisions.

Writing can be done in a formal journal, but it doesn't have to be. You can get the same benefits from using a journaling app on your phone, keeping a small notebook in your pocket or bag, or even jotting notes on a scrap of paper. Some people find it's useful to keep their writing and reread it at a later time. However, there's no need to save it if you prefer not to. Feel free to tear up or shred the papers or delete the computer files.

Keep in mind that the purpose of this writing is to help you recognize, clarify, and release your anger. It doesn't need to be neat, organized, or spell checked. You can simply write it as a stream of consciousness. If you have a hard time getting started, use some of the questions below, which incorporate some of the concepts from this chapter.

When did you first notice that you're feeling angry?

_____

_____

Describe how your anger feels in your body.

_____

_____

What feelings other than anger are you experiencing?

_____

_____

What do you think contributed to your feelings of anger?

_____

_____

Do you notice any unmet or unrealistic expectations that are contributing to your anger or stress?

_____

_____

What options do you see for resolving this issue?

_____

_____

What would make you feel better?

_____

_____

Talk It Out

Like writing, talking can have a cathartic effect. Talking about our feelings also offers added benefits when our anger is met with validation, reassurance, or hope from another person. When talking about anger (or any sensitive feeling or issue), it's important to choose a supportive person who can tolerate strong emotions and listen without judgment or offering unwanted advice. Unfortunately, talking may amplify our anger or leave us more frustrated if we aren't heard and supported, so we have to choose carefully whom to talk to. Often someone who isn't directly involved in the situation can be an objective listener.

Who are some safe people that you can talk to when you're angry?

_____

_____

Generally, we first need to vent our anger uncensored. Once we've released our feelings and talked about what happened that precipitated our anger, we might move on to exploring how our perfectionist thinking and expectations contributed to the problem.

Get Physical

Some people don't like to talk or write about their feelings, and that's okay. Many people find that they need a physical outlet for their anger. As we've discussed, anger often shows up in our bodies, so it makes sense that it also needs a physical release. Aerobic exercise, which raises our heart rate, such as running, dancing, or riding a bike, is particularly effective for decreasing anger. Sometimes, however, our environment, physical limitations, or preferences call for slower, quieter forms of exercise. Gentle stretching or yoga can feel wonderful on tense muscles. Another easy and convenient way to release anger is a progressive relaxation exercise. All you do is tighten the muscles in your toes for fifteen seconds and then release the muscles, then tighten the muscles in your feet for fifteen seconds and release, then your calf muscles, and systematically go through all the muscles in your body, tensing and releasing them. You can do this sitting, standing, or lying down.

A regular exercise routine is an important part of good physical and mental health for most people, so I encourage you to schedule regular times for physical activity. However, it's also good to have a repertoire of activities that you can do as needed—a spot treatment when your anger flares up. For example, sometimes you can't or don't want to take a yoga class, but perhaps you can close your office door for five minutes and get into the child's pose or do some side stretches. Or if you notice you're steaming after a conversation with your father, you might postpone running your errands and walk around the block instead. This is another great opportunity to challenge our all-or-nothing thinking! You don't need to run a 10K—just a few minutes of exercise can help you calm down and refocus.

What kinds of exercise do you do routinely? If you're not exercising regularly, what kind of exercise are you willing to try?

_____

_____

What physical activities will you do to help relieve anger in the moment? Remember to identify a number of strategies for different environments or situations.

_____

_____

_____

_____

Soothe Yourself

It's stressful and uncomfortable to remain in a state of anger: muscles are tense, thoughts are racing, and adrenaline is flooding our system. We feel better when we can soothe and calm ourselves, bring ourselves back to a state of inner peace and contentment.

Self-soothing is a skill that we develop as we grow up. Babies and toddlers have limited abilities to soothe themselves. They largely depend on their caregivers for comfort. So we swaddle and rock our little ones, sing lullabies to them, and give them baths with lavender soap in an effort to soothe them. Over time, children learn to calm themselves down when they're scared, hurt, or angry. But as we've been discussing, noticing and attending to our feelings isn't easy, and most adults struggle to do so to some degree. But with practice, we can home in on what feels comforting to us and learn to do things to calm ourselves and return to equilibrium. This doesn't necessarily mean that we've solved the source of our upset, but we'll be better equipped for problem solving from a state of calm.

Below is a list of things that feel comforting to some people. You can use these ideas as a starting place for creating your own list of comforting activities. Things that are particularly soothing are those that we've done in the past that have positive associations and things that have repetitive motions (this is why babies are soothed by rocking or walking). Keep that in mind as you create your list. You can circle the items below that you find comforting and add your own ideas.

- Sit in the sun.

- Do some yoga poses.

- Focus on taking slow, deep breaths.

- Take a hot bath or shower.

- Listen to your favorite music.

- Count to ten (or more!).

- Stretch.

- Meditate or just close your eyes and be still.

- Take a walk.

- Doodle, draw, or color.

- Write down ten things you're grateful for.

- Look at happy photos.

- Chew a piece of gum.

- Read an inspirational quote.

- Watch a funny video.

- Squeeze a stress ball.

- Savor a cup of tea.

- Focus on and really notice your present surroundings.

- Pet or play with your pets.

- Snuggle up with a loved one.

- Give yourself a hug or ask someone to give you one.

- _____

- _____

- _____

- _____

- _____

- _____

Summary

Feeling angry may seem like an imperfection, but it's completely normal. Sometimes it's the result of unmet expectations and our impossibly high perfectionist standards. As we discussed in this chapter, learning to notice our anger allows us to release it in more productive ways. We will continue to discuss anger and unmet expectations in the next chapter, in the form of criticizing others when they don't live up to our standards.

Chapter 10

From Criticizing to Accepting Others

In addition to being self-critical, many perfectionists are critical of others. This can cause problems in our relationships and contribute to feelings of low self-worth. It's also not an effective way to communicate. In this chapter, we're going to look at why some perfectionists are prone to criticizing, and how we can reduce that and learn to accept that others are imperfect too. Specifically, you'll learn to identify and change perfectionist thoughts that contribute to criticism, set realistic expectations, and use effective communication skills, such as the assertive communications skills we discussed in chapter 8, in order to positively communicate your needs and expectations and build more satisfying relationships.

Do You Hold Others to Unrealistically High Standards?

All perfectionists have unrealistically high standards for themselves. Many of us also have unrealistic expectations for others. When we expect our family members, coworkers, mechanics, and hairdressers to meet our impossibly high standards without fail or complaint, we often end up disappointed or frustrated. And our disappointment and frustration can result in our criticizing and nagging them.

Of course, criticism is an unproductive way to express our feelings and often contributes to relationship problems. We push people away, which makes them less interested in understanding and trying to meet our expectations.

What unrealistically high standards do you have for your spouse, children, friends, colleagues, or others?

_____

_____

_____

_____

_____

Criticism Deteriorates Relationships

When we expect perfection from others and are intolerant of mistakes, we can damage our relationships. Nagging, criticizing, and focusing on what our loved ones are doing wrong erodes connection and open communication. Quite simply, most people don't enjoy being around someone who is constantly complaining and pointing out their flaws. Let's take a look at Andrew and Carlos for an example of what can happen when criticism is frequent in a relationship.

Andrew and Carlos's Story

Andrew nitpicks his husband, Carlos, constantly. He finds fault with everything, from Carlos's career choice to how he folds the laundry. Andrew, a perfectionist, feels anxious about the uncertainty of Carlos's work as an aspiring novelist and his inattention to detail. Nearly every day, Andrew gives unwanted career advice or makes passive-aggressive comments about Carlos not having a steady paycheck or doing household chores up to par. "You're so inconsiderate! You were home all day and you still didn't get the oil changed in the car," he'll say, or he'll pester Carlos to get a "real job," insinuating that writing a book isn't really working.

Andrew feels frustrated that Carlos doesn't listen to him. Carlos never does what he asks, so why bother asking for help, he figures. Andrew's perfectionist thinking and unrealistic expectations of himself and Carlos keep him stuck in a pattern of criticizing Carlos and resenting Carlos for not living up to his standards or doing things the way he wants.

Just as self-criticism reflects our feelings of inadequacy, repeatedly criticizing others sends the message that we think they are inadequate or incompetent. Carlos, who's married to a critical perfectionist, feels like he's not good enough. It seems like Andrew notices only his imperfections and not his effort, improvement, and strengths. This is demoralizing. It feels like Andrew cares only about a steady paycheck and not about Carlos's dream of writing his novel. In response to Andrew's frequent criticism, Carlos put up an emotional wall; he tunes Andrew out and doesn't share things with him to protect himself from more criticism and hurt.

While Carlos responds with silence, other people respond to criticism from their partners or loved ones with criticism or anger of their own. According to renowned marriage researcher Dr. John Gottman, frequent criticism can lead to contempt or looking down on your partner with an air of superiority. And criticism and contempt are strong predictors of divorce (Gottman and Silver 2015).

How has criticizing negatively impacted your relationships?

_____

_____

_____

_____

_____

Criticizing Others Makes Us Unhappy

Criticism doesn't just have a negative impact on our relationships with others. It can also make us feel badly about ourselves. Many of us feel ashamed or guilty about our critical behaviors, because they don't align with our values and the perfect person we strive to be. We're also sensitive to criticism ourselves, so we know how hurtful it can be to be corrected, scolded, or critiqued.

Criticism also makes us unhappy because it tends to lead to more criticism, which leads to more feelings of guilt, regret, and self-reproach. As we discussed in chapter 5, we all have a negativity bias—we naturally tend to notice problems and discount the positives. Unfortunately, this is a prime set-up for criticizing, because it means it's easier to focus on what people are doing wrong than what they're doing right. For example, Carlos goes out of his way to do lots of helpful, caring things for Andrew, but many go unnoticed because the negativity bias predisposes Andrew to see Carlos's shortcomings, like not arranging an oil change for the car.

How do you feel when you criticize others?

_____

_____

_____

_____

Criticism Doesn't Motivate People

Earlier in the book, we worked on being kinder to ourselves because self-criticism doesn't motivate us to do better. The same is true when we criticize others; it tends to be demotivating and doesn't encourage people to listen to us or live up to our expectations. In fact, it can have the opposite effect, as it did on Carlos, who began to withdraw and tune his partner out due to his incessant criticism. Criticism often leaves people feeling ashamed, angry, or afraid rather than motivated.

How do others respond to your criticisms? Does it seem like an effective way to motivate and communicate?

_____

_____

_____

_____

Criticism often causes more problems than it solves. The next set of exercises will help you to anticipate situations in which you're likely to be critical, recognize and change thinking patterns that contribute to criticism, and set more realistic expectations.

Identify Your Triggers

You probably have certain people or situations that are triggers for criticism and nagging. Perhaps it's your employee who sends e-mails with typos to important customers or your child who never replaces the empty roll of toilet paper. For Andrew, seeing the bank statement triggers his perfectionism—an unrealistic belief that he should have a certain amount of money in the bank at all times and an underlying fear of not having enough.

When we repeatedly respond to the same things with criticism or anger, we reinforce these responses; in effect, they become hardwired in our brains. We heighten our sensitivity to the people or situations that trigger our criticism, so as soon as the situation arises, we're scanning for mistakes and unmet expectations. These hardwired responses to triggers can be changed as we create new ways of responding. To get started, identifying your triggers will help you anticipate challenging situations and prevent critical or angry responses.

What people or situations trigger you to criticize or nag?

_____

_____

_____

_____

_____

Perfectionist Thinking Leads to Criticism

Our tendency toward all-or-nothing thinking creates the unrealistic expectations that lead us to be overly critical of others. Our perfectionist thinking doesn't leave room for other people to make mistakes or have their own opinions, and it tends to assume the worst about people's actions and motives. Recognizing our perfectionist thoughts and reframing them can help us set realistic expectations and extend understanding and compassion when others are less than perfect.

Notice Perfectionist Thinking That Contributes to Criticism

Here are some examples of perfectionist thinking that can contribute to criticizing others. Check those that ring true for you and add additional examples at the bottom of the list.

☐ There's no excuse for mistakes.

☐ My way is the right way to do things.

☐ People always let me down. I can't count on anyone.

☐ If you want something done right, you have to do it yourself.

☐ If you don't listen to me, it means you don't care about me.

☐ If you don't follow through or complete a task, it's because you didn't really try.

☐ If I don't enforce some standards, this whole place will fall apart.

☐ People who make mistakes are careless, lazy, or inconsiderate.

☐ If I don't correct people, they'll never learn.

☐ _____

☐ _____

When you're aware of how your perfectionist thinking is contributing to being critical, you can start the process of challenging those thoughts and developing more realistic thoughts that are less judgmental and rigid.

Challenging Perfectionist Thinking

When we challenge our perfectionist thoughts, we question their validity and open ourselves to the possibility of thinking about ourselves, others, and situations from a different perspective. To get started, you might find it helpful to examine your own thinking:

• Am I taking someone else's behavior personally? Am I taking their behavior as a personal insult?

• Am I assuming the worst?

- Am I jumping to conclusions?

- Am I overreacting or being harsh?

- Is there more than one right way to do this?

- Can I see things from the other person's point of view?

Use the table below to practice challenging your perfectionist thoughts and replacing them with more realistic or positive thoughts.

Perfectionist thought	Challenge	Realistic or positive thought
Being late is unacceptable. Sam obviously doesn't care about me, or he wouldn't have been late.	*Perhaps there's another reason he was late. Instead of assuming he was late because he doesn't care about me, I could ask what happened.*	*Sometimes being late is unavoidable, and I can keep things in perspective and be more understanding.*

Setting Realistic Expectations

Now that you've noticed, challenged, and replaced some of your perfectionist thoughts, you can set realistic expectations. As we've discussed, we tend to set expectations that are so high that others can't consistently meet them, leaving everyone involved disappointed and unhappy. When this happens regularly, it's a clue that our expectations need to be adjusted.

It's okay to have some expectations, but we'll be most satisfied when we remember that people aren't always going to respond in ways that please us; they're imperfect too, and we can't make them do what we want. We can, however, control our expectations, and by making them realistic, we increase the chance that they'll be met. It can help to remember that adjusting your expectations isn't a cop-out or failure; it's a choice to be happier and more accepting of others.

Let's take another look at Andrew and Carlos. Andrew is particular about how and when he wants household chores to be done, but he now recognizes that criticizing Carlos about it is making both of them miserable. Andrew has a choice—he can't make Carlos do things his way, but he can change his expectations so that he's not critical and continuously disappointed.

The best way to figure out if your expectations are realistic or not is to pay attention to whether they are being met. Realistic expectations are those that others can meet most of the time—or come close to meeting. If you're consistently disappointed that someone isn't meeting an expectation, it is unrealistic to expect that they will meet it. It's important to distinguish between what you think someone *should* be able to do and what they actually do.

Try writing down some of the unrealistic expectations that you have about people you regularly interact with.

Person	Expectation	How often is this expectation met? (0–100 percent)
Sam	He'll always pick me up exactly at seven.	10 percent

Another thing to consider is whether your expectations align with your values. Sometimes we set expectations without thoughtfully considering whether they're really important to us. This might happen because we're comparing ourselves to others or because it's what we were taught and have just always done. For example, if your biggest criticism of your partner is tardiness, check in with yourself to see if punctuality is really one of your core values.

Do the expectations you identified reflect your values? (You can review the values you identified in chapter 7 to help.)

_____

_____

If you weren't so worried about what other people think, would you still set these expectations?

_____

_____

Sometimes we criticize others because we feel anxious and inadequate. When people don't respond the way we want or don't meet our expectations, we may feel out of control and flooded by fears of our own inadequacies. Criticizing others can become a way to temporarily regain a sense of control and release some of our nervous energy. This is why you may find yourself criticizing your spouse or children despite knowing full well that it doesn't get them to comply with your requests and that it leads to arguments and hurt feelings. In this case, we need a different kind of release valve and way to feel secure. Start by noticing what fears or stressors are behind your expectations. For example, Andrew's expectation that Carlos get a different job stems from his fears of not having enough money and being judged by family and friends who are financially better off.

What fears are underlying your expectations?

_____

_____

When you recognize that fears are contributing to your unrealistic expectations, you can take steps to calm yourself. Just taking three to five minutes to step away from the situation, take some slow, deep breaths, and repeat something like "I can remain calm" can calm your nervous system and slow down your thoughts so you can think about how you want to respond. The progressive relaxation exercise that we used in the last chapter—starting with flexing your toes for fifteen seconds, then relaxing, and moving up from one muscle group to the next—is another quick way to calm and center yourself.

Now that you've considered how often your expectations are met, whether they align with your values, and whether they are driven by fear and anxiety, you're ready to decide whether you think they're unrealistic.

Which of your expectations are unrealistic?

_____

_____

_____

_____

To adjust your expectations, rewrite them based on what actually happens or has happened in the past.

Unrealistic expectation	More realistic expectation
Sam will always pick me up exactly at seven.	*Sam will pick me up sometime between seven and seven fifteen.*

Creating more realistic expectations is an important part of increasing the chances that others can meet them. Learning to communicate them assertively will also increase the chances that others will meet our expectations.

Assertive Communication Is More Effective Than Criticism

Trying to reduce our criticism of others doesn't mean we can't ask for what we need, offer feedback, or correct people's work. Criticism, however, isn't the most effective way to communicate. Often criticism is reactive; we do it because we're frustrated or afraid and haven't thought through how or what we want to say. By using assertive communication, we can respond rather than react; we can give thoughtful consideration to the type and quantity of feedback we want to give and communicate it with respect.

Even when we communicate clearly and respectfully, we won't always get what we ask for, of course, but we're much more likely to have our needs and expectations met when we communicate them assertively. We can apply the same assertive communication skills presented in chapter 8 to provide feedback in a way that will be well received and promote an attitude of growth and change. We can provide feedback and ask for what we need in a respectful way that will both increase the chances of our message being heard and improve the quality of our relationships by giving others the benefit of the doubt and by expressing our care and concern.

Give Feedback Rather Than Criticism

To get our message across and preserve our relationships, it's helpful to make a distinction between criticism and feedback. Criticism tends to be angry, demanding, or degrading. It overgeneralizes someone's behavior or attacks their character. Feedback, on the other hand, isn't demanding or controlling. It offers information that can be helpful for change, gives encouragement, and is specific to an issue with someone's behavior rather than their character. Criticism is about calling attention to how bad or wrong we think someone is, whereas feedback is about finding a solution or way to move forward together. Criticism most often results in defensiveness, because it's blaming and judgmental. Feedback is more likely to be met with openness and cooperation. Assertive communication can help us express our needs or expectations about a specific situation or behavior without personally attacking others with global statements about their deficiencies. Here's an example to highlight the difference between criticism and feedback.

- Criticism: *You're always running up the credit card buying useless crap. You never think of anyone but yourself.*

- Feedback: *I'm feeling frustrated that there's a balance of $800 on the credit card. I see that you bought some things that I wasn't aware of. Let's go over our budget together and come up with a solution that will work for both of us.*

Constructive feedback uses many of the same assertive communication skills that we used in chapter 8. It's particularly helpful to remember these key points about assertive communication:

- Use I statements.

- Avoid generalities such as *always* or *never*.

- Focus on present behaviors.

- Use a calm tone.

- Demonstrate respect and cooperation rather than superiority and control.

Practice changing your criticisms into feedback.

Criticism	Feedback

Pick Your Battles

Although feedback can be useful, not every mistake or unfulfilled expectation that people make requires feedback from us. We need to decide when our feedback is likely to be welcome and when we're giving advice or corrections in an effort to control or quiet our own fears. Some people are simply not interested in feedback. Other times, if given the opportunity, people will self-correct; they'll notice their own errors and figure out how to improve on their own. Some people will let us know directly or indirectly that they aren't interested in feedback. If someone isn't showing signs that they're internally motivated to change, communicating our displeasure probably isn't going to motivate them.

Sometimes staying silent is the best option. It's a reflection that we're giving them the benefit of the doubt, allowing them to make their own choices, and accepting that they are imperfect. Before giving feedback or advice, try reflecting on your motives.

Why am I providing feedback? Do I have something constructive to add or am I trying to control or feel in charge?

_____

_____

_____

Look for What Others Do Right

Another powerful way to reduce criticism is to train ourselves to spot what people are doing right—whether big or small—and expressing it. We're less likely to criticize when we're focused on what someone's doing that's pleasing instead of scanning for their shortcomings. The negativity bias makes it easier for us to notice problems, but we can reprogram ourselves simply by practicing looking for what people do right. This exercise is straightforward, but it does take effort. The negativity bias is strong!

Write down five things that your family, friends, or workmates do right every day, and, if possible, tell the person what you noticed.

Person:	Expressed?
1.	
2.	
3.	
4.	
5.	

Person:	Expressed?
1.	
2.	
3.	
4.	
5.	

As you continue to notice what others are doing right, you'll probably feel more contentment and satisfaction in your relationships. And if you express your pleasure to others, it will help those around you to feel good about themselves and respond more positively to you.

Summary

Criticism doesn't have to ruin our relationships and cause us guilt and shame. As you've worked through the exercises in this chapter, you have taken the steps to change the perfectionist thinking that contributes to criticism, set realistic expectations, and communicate your expectations in a respectful and assertive way. You've also learned to shift your focus from what people are doing wrong to what they're doing right. The next challenge is to work on understanding how perfectionism leads us to feel guilty and how guilt can be a barrier to taking care of our physical, mental, and spiritual health.

Chapter 11

From Guilt to Self-Care

Throughout this book, we've been exploring the connection between perfectionism and self-worth and how our drive to please others and to perfect and prove ourselves can negatively affect our physical and mental health, relationships, and self-esteem. Self-care can ameliorate the effects of stress and prevent these types of negative effects, but as perfectionists, we tend to feel guilty about doing things for ourselves—anything that isn't a direct line to achieving a goal, meeting someone's expectations, or getting more done. Self-care doesn't fit our image of perfection; we think perfect people are self-sacrificing, low-maintenance, don't-need-anything types who can run on fumes and still get the job done. Because we have such unrealistic expectations of ourselves, we tend to underestimate our need for self-care and feel guilty about needing to rest, set boundaries, nurture our relationships, or have fun. But the reality is that we all need self-care. We have to tend to our physical, emotional, and spiritual needs in order to stay healthy and live a life that's fulfilling. In this chapter, we'll learn about the importance of self-care and how to practice it without feeling guilty.

What Is Self-Care?

Self-care is the practice of consistently taking care of our physical, emotional, or spiritual needs. It's doing something healthy and restorative for ourselves to help bring us back to health, contentment, and alignment with ourselves, others, and the world around us. Let's begin by taking a closer look at what self-care is and isn't, which will help you release guilt about doing things for yourself.

Self-Care Is Healthy, but Not Always Fun

Self-care is often confused with leisure, self-indulgence, or anything that's enjoyable. In fact, self-care isn't always enjoyable: going to the dentist is a form of self-care, because we're taking care of our health, but it's not particularly enjoyable. And conversely, not all enjoyable activities are self-care. Self-care is something that's good for us, so eating a bag of potato chips at the end of an excruciating day may be a treat, but it's not really self-care, because it's not a healthy way to take care of yourself, and it's not going to truly restore your physical or emotional energy.

This isn't to say that we need to make healthy choices all the time. We've all mindlessly eaten a bag of chips while binge-watching Netflix. It's fine for most of us to do this occasionally, and we don't need to criticize ourselves for it. We should just recognize that it's not quality self-care. Our efforts to practice self-care don't have to be perfect. Self-care is more about progress than perfection.

Self-Care Meets a Need

Another problem for perfectionists is that we often have unrealistic expectations of ourselves that create barriers to practicing self-care. Our perfectionist thinking convinces us that we shouldn't need anything, that we should be superhuman—able to work without getting tired, give without receiving, and achieve without effort. However, this isn't realistic—everyone has needs. And if we don't tend to our needs, we can't function optimally. We're used to pushing through, sucking it up, and doing things at any cost. Because of our perfectionism, most of us will sacrifice ourselves to make someone else happy or finish a project or attain a goal, but this isn't sustainable. Perhaps burnout, anxiety, or physical exhaustion led you to pick up this book. Meeting our needs through self-care is essential to our health and happiness. You may relate to Riya's story, which illustrates what happens when we consistently prioritize others' needs over our own.

Riya's Story

Riya is someone who will always help you out. If you're sick, she'll bring you a meal. If your car breaks down, she'll give you a ride. If you're behind at work, she'll stay late and pitch in. Riya puts everyone else's needs before her own. At her most recent physical exam, her doctor expressed concern about her high blood pressure and lack of sleep and encouraged her to take better care of herself. But Riya really didn't see the point. Sure, she's tired a lot, but her family and friends need her. She would feel guilty leaving her kids in daycare so she could go to the gym. She thinks she doesn't need a lunch break; she'll get more done if she works through lunch. She can make do with five hours of sleep. Even if she could find some quiet, taking a nap would seem lazy. She would feel selfish going out with friends after work instead of going straight home.

Self-care is an intentional activity done to meet a specific need, not just an excuse to lie around in our pajamas all day. Riya, like all of us, needs to exercise, eat lunch, get enough sleep, and socialize with friends. Doing these activities would meet her needs; they're not luxuries.

Our self-care is a way to meet our essential and normal physical, emotional, and spiritual needs. And because self-care is a needs-based practice, it's not a reward that we have to earn—nor is it selfish. It's something that we give to ourselves because we need it. Resting when you're tired is no different than eating when you're hungry, and yet we tend to judge ourselves negatively for resting and feel guilty about it.

Do you sacrifice your own needs to take care of, help, or please others? In what ways?

_____

_____

_____

_____

How does sacrificing your needs negatively affect you?

_____

_____

_____

_____

Misconceptions About Self-Care

In addition to the idea that self-care should always be fun, there are many other common misconceptions about self-care that create barriers to practicing it.

Which of these common misconceptions about self-care do you subscribe to?

Self-care is:

☐   a waste of time

☐   lazy

☐   selfish

☐   weak

☐   a sign of failure

☐   wrong

☐   expensive

☐   a reward I need to earn

☐   not important

☐   just the latest self-improvement fad

How do your misconceptions about self-care make it difficult for you to take care of yourself physically, emotionally, or spiritually?

_____

_____

_____

Now that you've recognized how some of your thinking may be limiting your self-care and contributing to exhaustion or resentment, you can begin to challenge your perfectionist thinking and create more positive thoughts about self-care and a plan for turning them into actions.

Challenging Perfectionist Thinking About Self-Care

Our misconceptions about self-care reflect our unrealistic expectations and rigid perfectionist thinking that labels things as "good" or "bad," "right" or "wrong." These thoughts create guilt or the feeling that we're doing something wrong when we practice self-care, so we tend to neglect our needs. To release our guilt, we need to challenge our perfectionist thinking about self-care to see if it's realistic and supportive of our goals to be happy and healthy.

Using the beliefs and expectations that you just identified, complete the chart below to challenge and replace perfectionist thoughts that get in the way of self-care.

Perfectionist or negative belief about self-care	Challenge	Realistic belief about self-care
Self-care is selfish.	Self-care meets needs, and everyone has needs.	It's healthy to care for myself.

Another way that you can challenge your guilt about self-care is to ask yourself if you're actually doing something wrong. As we discussed in chapter 5, often we find it easier to be compassionate and understanding of other people's needs than of our own So, you might ask yourself if you think it would be wrong for your best friend to practice self-care. For example, if you feel guilty about staying home from work when you've got a cold, ask yourself if you'd tell your friend that it's wrong to stay home sick. Consider whether you're holding yourself to a different standard—an unhealthy standard. Practice using this strategy below.

List a specific self-care activity that you feel guilty about.

_____

_____

What would you think if your best friend did this activity specifically to take care of his or her physical, mental, or spiritual health? Would you be understanding and supportive? Or would you say it's selfish or a waste of time?

_____

_____

Why is it wrong for you to do it? What perfectionist thoughts and misconceptions about self-care are contributing to your guilt?

_____

_____

Creating a Self-Care Plan

For most people, self-care requires effort, time, and planning. Like many things, we may have good intentions to practice self-care, but without a specific plan, it tends to fall to the bottom of the to-do list. Creating a plan that targets your unique needs will make it easier to identify and schedule activities that meet your needs and make self-care a priority.

Identifying What You Need

The first step in creating a self-care plan is to identify our needs. Our feelings and bodies are excellent at telling us what we need. Often we just need to slow down, be quiet, and listen to what they're telling us. You can build on the Noticing Your Feelings exercise that we've been using in this book to determine this:

- **How do I feel emotionally?** Name your feelings, being as descriptive as you can.

- **How does my body feel?** Notice things like pain, energy level, tension, heart rate, breathing, and so forth.

- **What do I need to bring myself back to wellness or contentment?** Use your feelings and body sensations to identify what you need.

Some common human needs are included in the following list. Feel free to adapt it to reflect your personal situation.

- food and water
- physical activity or exercise
- sleep
- rest or relaxation
- safety (physical and emotional)
- play or recreation
- belonging, social connection, and love
- emotional well-being or stability
- sense of purpose
- self-worth and a sense of competence
- self-determination or autonomy
- self-control

- self-expression or creativity

- connection to god, a higher power, the universe, or something larger than yourself

- learning, knowledge, or understanding

Fill in the following chart to identify what you need. You may find it helpful to use it two or three times per day.

Date and time	Feelings	Body sensations	Need
Monday morning	Anxious	Pounding head Stiff neck Tapping fingers Butterflies in my stomach	Relaxation

Once you've identified what you need, you're ready to decide how best to meet your needs.

Choosing Self-Care Activities

Finding self-care activities that work for you may take some experimenting, so try to keep an open mind and have patience while trying some different options. Also, remember that everyone practices self-care differently. I have listed some self-care ideas below just to get your ideas flowing. You are by no means limited to these activities. Some may appeal to you, but ultimately, you will create your own list of self-care activities that meet your needs and are effective, interesting, and practical for you.

- sit outside and enjoy nature
- have coffee with a friend
- do a guided meditation
- watch the sunrise or sunset
- journal
- color
- read a good book
- knit or crochet
- listen to a podcast
- take a nap
- deep breathing
- call a friend
- take a vacation day
- walk along the ocean
- blow bubbles
- pet your cat or dog
- take yourself out to lunch
- doodle
- cuddle with your partner
- speak up for yourself

- take a real lunch break during the workday
- go to a religious service
- go to bed on time
- write yourself a love letter
- do a crossword puzzle
- go to the library
- have a snack
- do just one thing at a time
- take photos
- sit in silence and do nothing
- reread a favorite book from childhood
- feed the ducks
- say no to something you don't want to do
- stargaze
- take a class because you want to
- have a family game night
- take a bubble bath
- pray

- talk to a therapist
- take medication as prescribed
- eat a healthy meal
- pick flowers in your garden
- crank up the music and sing along
- practice yoga
- watch a funny YouTube video
- play the piano, guitar, or another instrument
- dance
- bike ride
- light a scented candle or diffuse essential oils
- play with your dog
- hike
- pull weeds in your garden or water your plants
- make something

Although we all need to find the self-care activities that work for us, I recommend trying to choose activities that are mindful rather than mindless. For example, spending thirty minutes mindlessly scrolling through social media is an easy distraction, and most people assume it's self-care because it's not productive work. However, many people actually feel worse after spending time on social media—often because they're comparing themselves to others or getting riled up by political arguments or other tense conversations. Using social media or watching television isn't necessarily a bad thing, but if they leave you feeling drained, they're probably a distraction rather than a true form of self-care. Sometimes the same activity can be done either mindfully or mindlessly. You could take a hot shower and savor the experience, noticing how good it feels on your sore muscles and purposefully enjoying the smell of the shampoo and warmth of the water, or you could rush through your shower, distracted by everything you have to do today and criticizing your jiggly thighs or thinning hair. The first shower experience is more restorative. When we mindfully engage in self-care, using our senses to tune in to the full experience, we can maximize the benefits.

You might find it useful to use the chart below to organize your self-care activities according to the needs they meet. Some activities may meet multiple needs. For example, doing yoga could meet your need for exercise, relaxation, emotional well-being, and connection to a higher power.

Need	Possible self-care activities

Putting Your Plan into Action

So far, we've talked about meeting our needs as they occur. We can also practice self-care pro-actively—anticipating what we will need. You may notice patterns about your needs, such as feeling stressed and overwhelmed when you get home from work. This can help you establish routines to meet needs that you can reasonably predict. To meet your need for relaxation when you get home from work, you might establish a practice of meditating or savoring a cup of decaffeinated tea at the end of every workday. Healthy habits are a particularly important part of a self-care plan, because habits and routines make it quicker and easier for us to make healthy choices, and being proactive can help us meet needs before they become greater and potentially more difficult to meet.

Many people like to create a weekly self-care plan based on their anticipated needs. Taking the extra step of scheduling time (and budgeting money, if necessary) also makes it easier to follow through on a self-care plan. I use a worksheet like the one on the following page and then write specific self-care activities on my calendar. It doesn't address every need I may have, but it helps ensure that I'll meet my most important needs. If you find this worksheet helpful, you can access additional copies, called "Self-Care Plan," at http://www.newharbinger.com/41535.

Giving Yourself Permission

There's one final step to implementing a guilt-free self-care plan: giving yourself permission. Formally telling yourself that you need and deserve self-care can make the difference between following through on your plan or not. Giving yourself permission solidifies your commitment to recognizing that your needs are important, valid, and deserve to be met.

I give myself permission to _____ as a way of taking care of myself.

I give myself permission to _____ as a way of taking care of myself.

Self-Care Plan

	Sunday	Monday	Tuesday	Wednesday	Thursday	Friday	Saturday
I will care for my body by:							
I will care for my spirit by:							
I will care for my emotional health by:							
I will care for my need for social connection by:							
I will show myself love by:							

Summary

Most people agree that self-care is essential to our well-being, but it's not always easy to do. This chapter has addressed ways to break through the guilt that prevents many perfectionists from practicing self-care. When we challenge our perfectionist thinking, we can let go of our misconceptions about self-care and unrealistic expectations of ourselves. This allows us to acknowledge our needs, choose self-care activities to meet those needs, make a self-care plan, and give ourselves permission to carry it out. Next, we're going to be taking a look at shame, which is perhaps the true root of perfectionism, and how it fuels perfectionism and our intense drive to prove our worth.

Chapter 12

From Shame to Connection

Shame is another feeling that perfectionists know well—the feeling that we're fundamentally flawed and inadequate. Our obsession with achievements, pleasing, and perfect appearances are all efforts to compensate for feeling ashamed and afraid of rejection. Shame is a painful emotion, so it's understandable that we will do everything in our power to avoid it. You may be tempted to skip this chapter and not tackle the pain associated with shame, or you may not be aware that shame is negatively impacting you, but I encourage you to give it a try, because the rewards are great. In this chapter, I'm going to help you understand the role shame plays in perfectionism, how shame leads to disconnection, and ways to reduce our feelings of shame so we can connect with ourselves and others in meaningful ways. Although it's difficult, learning to deal with shame can be instrumental in overcoming perfectionism.

Shame Creates Perfectionism and Perfectionism Creates Shame

Shame is the driving force behind perfectionism. As I said, shame reflects a belief that there's something wrong with us, not just that we've done something wrong, and it leads us to overcompensate with perfectionism. For perfectionists, shame is essentially the intolerable experience of being imperfect.

Perfectionists tend to experience high levels of shame as part of our "I'm unworthy and need to prove myself" mentality. We then create more shame with our unrealistically high self-expectations. We set impossible standards, fail to meet them (because they're completely unrealistic), blame ourselves, and feel ashamed. This experience looks something like this:

Shame (belief that I'm flawed) →perfectionism → impossibly high standards → failure → self-blame → shame

And the cycle repeats because our feelings of shame and unworthiness lead us to perfectionism and trying to prove our worth through impossible achievements. Unlike others, we don't see failure as a healthy part of growth and development. We see it as proof of our inferiority, and it further reinforces our shameful feelings.

How have your perfectionism, fear of failure, and unrealistically high standards contributed to feelings of shame?

_____

_____

_____

_____

_____

Now that we understand the synergistic relationship between shame and perfectionism, let's turn our attention to how you can identify shame in your own life.

Identifying Shame

Feelings of shame come from being judged as unacceptable by others or from doing something that we believe will be judged harshly by others and that isn't acceptable in our community's norms. We internalize this judgment as an indication that *we* are unacceptable, not our actions. The things that cause us to feel ashamed are closely related to our perfectionist fears. In chapter 4, we explored common perfectionist fears, such as the fear of failure, rejection, judgment, criticism, not being liked, and not being good enough. Take a look back at the fears that you identified, as they will likely help you identify sources of shame. For example, if you identified a fear of failure, doing something that you perceive as a failure will probably cause you to feel ashamed.

Take a moment now and jot down the fears you identified in chapter 4.

_____

_____

_____

Linda's story also demonstrates the connection between her perfectionism, fears, and shame.

Linda's Story

Linda, thirty-two, had mapped out her life in childhood. After high school, she would go to culinary school, become a pastry chef, get married, have two children, and eventually open her own high-end bakery. From an early age, she knew she was in her older brother's shadow. He was clearly their parents' favorite child, which left Linda fearing she wasn't good enough. So Linda tried to surpass her brother's accomplishments, and her success was impressive. She was working as the head pastry chef in an acclaimed New York City restaurant. And she'd been happily married to Nigel for five years before she visited a reproductive endocrinologist and was diagnosed with endometriosis, which was causing her infertility. Linda was devastated, as was Nigel. But Linda blamed herself. She felt defective and inferior for not being able to get pregnant—something other women do so easily, even accidentally. As unsuccessful infertility treatments ensued, Linda felt more and more like a failure as a woman and a wife. She feared Nigel would leave her for a woman who could bear him children, although he reassured her that he loved her more than ever. Linda felt deep shame about her infertility. She refused to confide in her friends and family. She needed to maintain a perfect façade, busying herself with work and telling others that she was focused on her professional goals and not interested in having children.

Your shame story may be very different than Linda's, but we all have one. And it can be very painful to acknowledge the things we feel ashamed of. As we begin this process, be sure to practice self-compassion (refer back to chapter 5 for a refresher) and work slowly so you don't overwhelm yourself. This may also be a helpful place to work with a psychotherapist if difficult feelings and memories emerge.

Below is a list of things that often cause feelings of shame. What causes shame for each of us is unique to us, of course, but these may help you start to identify shame in your life:

- getting divorced

- abusing drugs or alcohol

- having a mental illness

- having an abortion

- having a family history of poverty, addiction, mental illness, or criminal activity

- watching pornography

- being abused or being abusive

- being fired

- your appearance

- being infertile

- being arrested

- being in debt

- having an affair

- placing a child for adoption

- having a learning disability

- doing something that goes against your values or morals

In addition to being able to identify the events that trigger shame, we want to be able to identify the thoughts and physical sensations of shame. Often our bodies give us the first cues that something is off. In the case of shame, we may be reluctant to acknowledge the sources of our shame, because they're so painful, so noticing our self-critical thoughts and physical symptoms can be an easier place to begin.

Linda's shame-filled thoughts included: *I'm a failure as a woman. I'm a terrible wife. My husband will leave me. I have nothing to give. I'm worthless.* You'll notice that these are distorted and catastrophic thoughts that reflect Linda's experience of being imperfect (being unable to conceive a child). As I mentioned earlier, perfectionists are particularly vulnerable to shame because of our unrealistic expectations. In addition to her thoughts, Linda could identify many of the common physical symptoms of stress, such as headaches, fatigue, clenching her teeth, and irritability, which also indicated that she was experiencing shame.

How do you know when you're experiencing shame? What thoughts and physical sensations do you experience?

_____

_____

_____

_____

_____

To explore shame more deeply, try to write about at least one source of shame. What unfilled expectations of yourself contribute to feeling ashamed? How does this situation make you feel defective or inadequate?

_____

_____

_____

_____

_____

_____

The Painful Effects of Shame

Shame is a very painful experience—much more painful than guilt or embarrassment—because it reflects a belief that we *are* unacceptable or unworthy, rather than a belief that we *did* something unacceptable. When we experience shame, we feel flawed at our core and unlovable, which is why all of our efforts to behave and appear perfect can't rid us of shame. Shame is a belief about who we are as people.

Most people keep their shame concealed. We don't generally talk about the things we're ashamed of, because they reflect our feelings of unworthiness and fears of judgment and rejection. The effects of shame can be profound; shame is associated with aggression, bullying, violence, addiction, eating disorders, and depression (Brown 2012). And the results of holding in these negative beliefs and fears can be devastating. They eat away at our self-esteem and negatively impact our relationships, because shame can make us guarded, distant, and afraid of judgment.

How does shame negatively impact your behavior, thoughts, and physical and emotional health?

_____

_____

_____

_____

_____

Disconnection is one of the most painful repercussions of shame. In the next section, we'll take a closer look at how shame causes us to feel disconnected and alone and how overcoming shame can help us build closer connections.

Shame Creates Disconnection

In her book *Daring Greatly*, Brené Brown writes: "Shame is the fear of disconnection—it's the fear that something we've done or failed to do, an ideal that we've not lived up to, or a goal that we've not accomplished makes us unworthy of connection" (2012, 68–69). We might rewrite this idea as:

shame is the fear that being imperfect makes us unlovable and unworthy of connection. So when we experience shame, we go to extreme lengths to try to be perfect, because we believe perfection is our ticket to love and belonging. But this is a false belief; trying to be perfect isn't actually going to help us build connection—often it does the opposite.

As perfectionists, we strongly resist sharing our insecurities and imperfections with others. This leads to disconnection, because when we don't share our feelings and experiences—the good and the bad—we feel alone. And if we aren't having conversations that include sharing mistakes and imperfections, we tend to fill in the gaps with assumptions. For example, if my sisters and friends don't confide in me that they have made mistakes or had difficult things happen in their lives, I'm apt to assume that they have it all together and that I'm the only one who's experienced difficulties—because I'm inferior. Of course, this is an inaccurate assumption; everyone has regrets, family secrets, and flaws of various kinds. But when we get stuck in shame, we imagine either that other people don't have any failings or that they aren't as bad as ours. We conclude that we're outliers. This is how shame builds walls among us. We're each in our own shame bubble—isolated, afraid of judgment, and feeling completely unworthy—so we remain silent and don't share our imperfections. Patrick's story exemplifies how the belief that we're different and inferior not only pushes us toward perfectionism but also causes us to be emotionally distant from others.

Patrick's Story

Patrick, fifty, came to see me for therapy because his marriage was falling apart. He told me that he and his wife had had communication problems from the beginning and had grown apart over the years, but now she had moved out, and Patrick was worried that his wife would ask him for a divorce. Patrick, a stoic man born in Ireland, had been a hardworking and successful software engineer in Silicon Valley for the past twenty years. Work had often been his retreat when things were difficult at home. Patrick's wife complained that he didn't share his feelings with her; he couldn't be vulnerable and let her into his inner world. Through our sessions, it became apparent that this was true. Even after twenty-five years together, Patrick was afraid to tell his wife about the deep shame he felt about his childhood. Patrick had been sexually abused by his grandfather until he was twelve years old. He had never told anyone. Not his parents. Not his sister. Not his best friend. Not his wife. He buried it and tried to pretend it didn't affect him. But it was this deep shame and the core belief that he was unlovable and unworthy that drove him to overwork, and it's also what built a wall between him and his wife. He feared she'd look at him differently—she wouldn't respect and love him—if she knew about the abuse he suffered as a child. Shame about being sexually abused led to his perfectionist thinking and the dissolution of his marriage.

How does shame or the fear of being unworthy and unlovable keep you separate or disconnected? Has it contributed to missed opportunities for connection or the breakdown of relationships?

_____

_____

_____

_____

_____

Now that we've examined how shame is a barrier to deep connection and intimacy, we'll turn our attention to how we can decrease our shame and start to build stronger connections.

Decreasing Shame and Building Connection

We can decrease shame and build connection with others by learning to be more authentic. Authenticity decreases shame because it allows us to feel fully accepted for who we are, including the things we're ashamed of. And as our shame decreases and our authenticity increases, our ability to connect with others also improves.

Connection Requires Vulnerability

We can only connect deeply with others when we allow ourselves to be authentic. And authenticity requires us to be vulnerable—to be fully seen. Since we've spent our lives invested in trying to be perfect as a way to prove our worth, it's challenging for us to let our guard down and allow others to know us more openly, especially our messy, imperfect parts.

As we've discussed, shame is what prevents perfectionists from being vulnerable. When we try to step out of perfectionism, shame rears its head and dissuades us from being authentic. Shame tells us that we're wrong, bad, and worthless. We fear criticism for our imperfections and imagine that others will judge us harshly. The voice of shame might sound like this: _What will Joe think if I tell him I got a DUI? I'm sure he'll think I'm an awful person. I better not tell him. I can't risk his disapproval._

So, instead, we retreat to the safety of perfectionism. Our perfectionist thinking tells us that if we appear perfect, people won't reject, judge, or criticize us. We imagine that being perfect will ensure that we're accepted and loved. The problem is that people can't like us if they don't know us. And knowing our accomplishments and the trappings of our successes isn't really knowing us. These are only tiny fractions of who we are. As we've discussed in this workbook, we're much more than a resume, title, or the bio on a website. Deep connection happens when people know about our mistakes and secrets—and they like us anyway.

We can begin the process of being more vulnerable by identifying safe people to begin to open up to. We don't need to share our personal experiences of imperfection with just anyone. We want to carefully select those who have shown they're trustworthy and empathetic. In addition to friends and family members, you might consider practicing vulnerability with a therapist, clergy member or spiritual leader, mentor, or support group.

Whom can you begin to share your imperfections with?

_____

_____

_____

_____

We also want to start to share more of ourselves through incremental steps. For example, you're not going to lead with your biggest source of shame (for Linda, her infertility, and for Patrick, being a victim of childhood sexual abuse). Instead, you'll start by sharing a mistake or imperfection that you feel a small amount of shame about, like your credit card being declined, gossiping about a coworker, or leaving dirty coffee mugs in the office sink and never washing them.

What are some of the smaller sources of shame that you might begin to share?

_____

_____

_____

_____

As you begin to talk about your shame with others, pay attention to the responses you get. This will inform your decision about whether to share more or not. Receiving an empathetic response to shame is what heals it.

Empathy Builds Connection

Empathy is understanding and sharing how someone else is feeling. It conveys that I'm feeling (sadness, anger, or another emotion) *with* you, unlike sympathy, which means I'm feeling sadness or pity *for* you. When we empathize, we can take someone else's perspective and understand their feelings without judgment. Empathy makes us feel connected because it affirms that we aren't alone in our struggles. It doesn't invalidate or try to change our feelings, such as trying to cheer us up when we're sad. Empathy shows acceptance of our feelings, experiences, and who we are. When Linda shared that her in-vitro fertilization (IVF) was unsuccessful, she received an empathetic response from her best friend and a sympathetic response from her sister.

- Empathetic response: *Oh, Linda, I'm so sorry the IVF procedure didn't work. I know you've been trying to get pregnant for such a long time. It sounds so painful and frustrating and disappointing. I want to hear what it's been like for you.*

- Sympathetic response: *I'm sorry to hear that. Stay positive! I'm sure it will work next time!*

An empathetic response brings people closer.

Think about something vulnerable that you've shared or would like to share, write an example of an empathetic response that would feel good to you.

_____

_____

Often when we share something that's shameful or vulnerable, the other person will share their own shameful experience in return. When this is done in an empathetic way—not a comparative or one-upmanship type of way—it builds connection by reinforcing our shared experiences of being imperfect. We get the feeling not only that we're understood but also that we're all struggling together and that none of us is perfect.

So when someone opens up to you, you have the opportunity to reciprocate in sharing something vulnerable and building a deeper connection. Here's an example of how this might happen when someone begins to share a small piece of their shame.

Mark: "I completely blew it. I scheduled a new client for eight o'clock this morning, and I forgot all about the appointment. He got to my office, and no one was there! I feel like such a loser. I'm the worst therapist ever. Why would anyone want to hire me?"

Me: "Wow, that sucks. I know how hard you've worked to start the clinic and build a good reputation. I can understand why you're so frustrated with yourself. That sounds really upsetting."

Mark: "Yeah, I can be so stupid!"

Me: "Well, we all do things like that sometimes. It's not just you! When I was teaching Intro to Psych last semester, I forgot the final exam. Can you believe that? I was in such a rush that morning that I left the whole stack of exams on the copy machine and didn't even realize it until I got to class. Everyone was asking, 'Where's the exam?' I felt like such a fraud. I just kept thinking, *Whatever made me think I could do this?*"

Mark: "I didn't know that. That must have been awful!"

In this example, I took the opportunity to share something that I was ashamed of with Mark not to make it all about me, but to normalize his experience and let him know that I'm not perfect either.

How does it feel when someone shares something vulnerable with you?

_____

_____

Are you more likely to share something vulnerable in return?

_____

_____

How can you encourage others to be vulnerable with you?

_____

_____

Of course, your efforts to be more authentic and vulnerable may not always be met with empathy and shared vulnerability. With that in mind, consider how you will cope with such a situation. Perhaps refer back to chapter 11 for some self-care ideas.

How will you cope if your efforts to connect aren't reciprocated or your vulnerability isn't met with empathy?

_____

_____

_____

As I mentioned, learning to talk about shame is a difficult process and not one to undertake too quickly. I encourage you to work through the exercises in this chapter repeatedly and pay attention to how you feel as you practice sharing more of your authentic self.

Summary

In this chapter, we identified the connection between shame and perfectionism—specifically that perfectionists are susceptible to shame because we believe we're inherently unworthy, which leads us to set unattainable goals and unrealistically high expectations that we can't fulfill, leaving us feeling more ashamed. We also discussed how shame isolates us and becomes a barrier to authentic connection with others. We can decrease our shame and create more fulfilling and intimate relationships by learning to share our imperfections—the source of our shame—with people who are likely to provide empathy and acceptance. In the final chapter, we'll discuss how to stay motivated, how to maintain the changes you've made thus far, and ongoing ways to practice accepting your imperfections.

Chapter 13

Putting It All Together

You're nearing the end of *The Perfectionism Workbook*, and even if you've completed all of the exercises and reflective questions in this book, your perfectionism may still be rearing its head and getting in your way. This is completely normal! It doesn't mean you've done something wrong or that these exercises don't work. Most of the exercises in this book are designed to be repeated for maximum benefit; doing them only once is unlikely to give you the results you're looking for. So in this chapter, you will learn how to deal with some of the common pitfalls of self-improvement efforts—getting discouraged and sliding back into old behaviors. To avoid these, we'll discuss ways to cope with feeling discouraged and how to maintain the progress you've already made. This chapter will include using strategies we've already discussed, such as self-compassion, partial successes, setting realistic expectations, and self-care. And you'll learn how to visualize success, identify where to focus your practice efforts, and create a practice routine.

Staying Motivated

Changing long-standing behavior and thought patterns is a process. Often it's not a straight path, but rather a bumpy road with unexpected setbacks, change attempts that don't seem to go anywhere, and efforts that stall out. This can be disheartening, especially because our perfectionist nature wants change to happen seamlessly and easily. But as we've discussed throughout this book, setbacks and mistakes aren't failures, they're important opportunities to learn something new. Staying motivated is an important part of any change plan, and many of the strategies we've used throughout this book can help.

Self-Compassion

It's very easy, especially for perfectionists, to become self-critical when we don't behave the way we want and when our efforts to change aren't quick and easy. Many perfectionists feel disappointed or angry with themselves for not being able to change—or "fix"—their perfectionism, especially after putting in a lot of effort.

Have there been times, as you've worked through this book, that you've felt discouraged or like you're not making progress? Explain what this has been like for you.

Example: *Changing has been so much harder than I thought. I can't seem to stop criticizing my family. I love them, and I know I'm hurting them. I'm so angry with myself for acting like this, and I'm doubting whether I can ever change.*

_____

_____

_____

_____

_____

Your old pattern was probably to respond to these experiences with self-criticism—to blame yourself for not working hard enough or being smart enough. But as we discussed in chapter 5, self-criticism doesn't generally motivate us, it makes us feel more ashamed and worthless. Self-compassion is a tool that can be helpful when you're feeling frustrated or discouraged with the change process.

Using the tenets of self-compassion, what can you say to yourself to acknowledge your struggle, normalize it, and respond with compassion?

Example: *Change is hard. And it's a long process. I've been working hard on this, and it means a lot to me; it's normal to feel frustrated. The fact that I haven't mastered this skill doesn't mean I'm doing something wrong.*

_____

_____

   Try to notice when self-criticism returns, and instead of seeing it as a failure, use it as an opportunity to practice giving yourself the same loving kindness that you give to others. This will help you calm and soothe yourself so that you can put things in perspective and realize that change is a process of baby steps that you make every day.

Partial Successes

   The strategy of partial successes (chapter 6) is a great way to reframe our all-or-nothing thinking and a helpful tool for staying motivated. Focusing on everything you're doing wrong is demotivating. Instead, partial successes help us to see the effort and progress we've made and recognize that it counts even if it's imperfect or incomplete.

   Try reframing as a partial success something that felt like a failed effort to change or a discouraging experience in your journey to overcome perfectionism. Below there are two examples. The first shows a partial success directly related to the specific struggle (in this case, anger and criticizing others), and the second example shows a partial success related to the larger goal of reducing perfectionism. If you have trouble identifying a specific partial success, you can choose a more general one.

Perceived failure or challenge: *This morning, I yelled at my kids three times to clean up their shoes and jackets, and I criticized my son for getting up late.*

Partial success: *After school I noticed that my son did his homework without prompting, and I praised him for this.*

Partial success: *I wrote in my gratitude journal for seven consecutive days.*

Perceived failure or challenge: _____

_____

Partial success: _____

_____

Perceived failure or challenge: _____

_____

Partial success: _____

_____

Realistic Expectations

One of the strongholds of our perfectionism is setting exceptionally high expectations of ourselves. This essentially sets us up to feel like we're failing, because it's impossible to meet these expectations. And having unrealistic expectations about how much we can change, and how quickly and effortlessly we can do it, often leads to discouragement and demotivation.

Many people find it helpful to recall that they have been reinforcing their perfectionist thinking and behaviors for _____ (fill in your age) years, and it's not realistic to completely eliminate these tendencies in six months or a year. This helps keep things in perspective and bring our expectations back to reality.

Another tool that I've mentioned in this book is the mindset "progress not perfection," which reminds you that your objective isn't to completely eliminate all of your perfectionist thoughts and behaviors. It's tempting to want to strive for 100 percent elimination of these troublesome tendencies, but it's not realistic for most of us. Nor is it the only way to experience the benefits of reducing your perfectionism.

How has your life already improved because of the progress you've made in reducing your perfectionism? Consider your physical and mental health, work-life balance, willingness to try new things and take chances, and relationships.

_____

_____

_____

_____

_____

For most people, even a modest reduction in their perfectionism will lead to meaningful positive changes in their life. Because of the negativity bias, sometimes the hardest part is actually recognizing your progress and celebrating it. If you choose to continue keeping a gratitude journal, try including your efforts to change and the positive results that you're experiencing, which will reinforce them.

Visualize Success

Another way to stay motivated and think positively about the change process is to visualize yourself acting in new ways. This creates a mental picture of success that strengthens your confidence. This technique is most helpful when you visualize changing what you can control (yourself) rather than visualizing yourself achieving a particular outcome. For example, try visualizing yourself practicing assertive communication at work instead of visualizing yourself getting a raise, which you can't completely control. Use the steps below to get started with visualizing a successful change process.

1. Think of a particular change you want to make.

2. Identify the barriers or challenges you face in making this change.

3. Find a quiet place to sit.

4. Relax your body and close your eyes.

5. Imagine yourself making this change, overcoming the barrier or challenge, and acting in the desired way. Describe the scene to yourself in as much detail as possible. Try to use all of your senses. Who or what do you see? What do you hear? What are the facial expressions of the people you are with? What are you doing? How do you feel? How do you overcome the barriers?

You can also describe the situation in writing in the space provided.

_____

_____

_____

_____

Most people find that visualization works best when they repeat it regularly.

Increase Your Self-Care

As we discussed in chapter 11, self-care is taking care of our physical, emotional, and spiritual needs. It's worth revisiting here, because when we ask a lot of ourselves, we also need to give a lot to ourselves. It takes a lot of time and energy to read and complete this workbook and apply the concepts consistently in your life. In order to do this, you need to be consistently replenishing yourself, or you'll quickly become depleted, which can lead to procrastination, avoidance, frustration, and discouragement. If you notice these feelings creeping in, it's a cue to increase your self-care.

What's one healthy, positive thing you can do for yourself when you feel discouraged about your progress?

_____

_____

You may also find it useful to print out another Self-Care Plan (available at http://www .newharbinger.com/41535) for a more structured approach to taking care of your needs.

In addition to staying motivated, people often struggle to maintain the changes they achieved. Maintaining change requires ongoing practice and planning, which we'll turn our attention to now.

Maintaining Change

When making significant changes, it's not uncommon for people to slip back into old patterns from time to time. It takes substantial effort not only to make but also to maintain changes in our thoughts and behaviors. After completing all of the exercises in this book, you've hopefully learned a great deal about yourself and about specific ways to overcome perfectionism. Practice is the key to maintaining these changes.

Continue to Use This Book

We all need ongoing practice to maintain the progress we've made. For example, after training for and running a marathon, you couldn't stop training and expect to maintain all of the gains you'd made. We all accept that to remain physically fit, we need to continue the practices that helped us become fit. Maintaining the gains you've made in overcoming perfectionism is no different; it requires ongoing practice. The new ways of thinking and acting that you've learned from *The Perfectionism Workbook* will get easier and feel more natural the more that you practice them. So it's a good investment of time and energy to set up a plan for ongoing practice.

Reinforcing Concepts

Now is a good opportunity to reflect on the progress you've made and identify which areas of your perfectionism need more of your attention. In chapter 2, you identified your perfectionist traits and how perfectionism was negatively impacting your physical health; emotional well-being; ability to prioritize work, personal interests, and needs; pursue new opportunities; and have satisfying relationships. It may be helpful to reflect back on your answers in those sections and then answer the questions below. Again, remember that it's completely normal to still be struggling with perfectionist thoughts and behaviors.

Which areas of your life continue to be negatively impacted by perfectionism?

_____

_____

_____

_____

Which of these areas do you feel most motivated to continue working on?

_____

_____

_____

_____

Continuing to work on the exercises in this book that were challenging the first time through can also be beneficial, as can repeating the exercises that seemed to give you the best results.

Which chapters or exercises in this book were the most challenging?

_____

_____

_____

_____

Which provided the greatest insights or growth?

_____

_____

_____

_____

Identifying the areas that you'd like to continue to improve in, as well as the exercises that were especially challenging or beneficial, will help you to focus your practice on the areas that will be most useful and keep it manageable. Continuing to practice is likely to further reduce the negative impact of perfectionism in your life.

Create a Routine

Routines make it easier for us to do things that are good for us or that are in alignment with our goals and values. When we do the same thing at the same time each day, for example, it takes less effort than if we have to decide when and how and even if we're going to do something. Things are more likely to get done if we put a consistent plan in place. When we set things up as optional—waiting until we have time or we feel like doing them—it's easy to procrastinate or not do them at all. So creating a routine will help you prioritize practicing the skills you've learned in this book.

Being realistic about your time and energy, how much time can you commit to practicing each week?

_____

Which chapters or exercises will you focus on this week?

_____

_____

_____

Open your calendar, journal, or whatever tool you use to keep track of your schedule and record when you will do each exercise and for how long. Sticking to a routine will make it easier.

Sample Practice Schedule

Sunday	8:00–8:30 Challenging My Negative Thoughts (chapter 4) 10:00–10:15 Gratitude Journal (chapter 7)
Monday	10:00–10:15 Gratitude Journal
Tuesday	10:00–10:15 Gratitude Journal
Wednesday	8:00–8:30 Noticing Perfectionist Thinking That Contributes to Criticism; Challenging Perfectionist Thinking (chapter 10) 10:00–10:15 Gratitude Journal
Thursday	10:00–10:15 Gratitude Journal
Friday	10:00–10:15 Gratitude Journal
Saturday	10:00–10:15 Gratitude Journal

A good rule of thumb is to practice using the routine you've decided upon for thirty days and then reevaluate whether more or less practice is needed. Over time, as your perfectionist tendencies lessen, you'll be able to decrease your practice time, so you won't have to practice at this level forever. However, you're most likely to maintain the changes you've made if you incorporate at least some of the strategies and exercises into a routine that you maintain indefinitely.

Practice Being Imperfect

Being able to accept our imperfections and recognize that we're worthwhile people despite them is our ultimate goal in overcoming perfectionism. For years, our perfectionism has told us that imperfections are unacceptable and that we should deny them, be ashamed of them, and go to extraordinary lengths to correct them. When we embrace our imperfections, we don't have to earn our worth or feel bad about being less than perfect. While there may still be things we want to change about ourselves, we can practice accepting ourselves just as we are right now. To reinforce that being imperfect is normal and acceptable, try using the exercise below.

Write down your imperfections or mistakes you have made in the left-hand column, and then write a statement accepting these things.

Imperfection or mistake	Statement of acceptance
I'm overweight.	*I accept my body the way it is. I don't have to be a size 2 to have worth.*
I overcommitted myself, got stressed out, and snapped at my coworker.	*I accept that I'm imperfect and sometimes make mistakes like overcommitting myself and losing my temper. This doesn't mean I'm less of a person.*

In addition to practicing ways to change your perfectionist thinking and behavior, accepting your imperfections can be a powerful way to boost your confidence and mood, and this will help keep you on the path to overcoming perfectionism.

Summary

Overcoming perfectionism is a process. Completing this workbook is a big step in making changes to your perfectionist thoughts and behaviors and creating happy, fulfilling relationships, but it's not the end of the journey. You may find it useful to continue to use the exercises in this book—consistently practicing them or returning to them as needed. In particular, self-compassion, noticing partial successes, setting realistic expectations, visualizing success, and practicing self-care can help you stay motivated. Continuing to practice these concepts and implementing them in your life will give you the freedom to be imperfect—to be your authentic self.

Appendix A

Cognitive Distortions

All-or-nothing thinking	You see things as absolutes, with no in-betweens. Example: *I'm stupid.*
Mind reading	You assume others are thinking the same thing you are. Example: *I'm sure I didn't get the job because I'm too old.*
Double standard	You hold yourself to a higher standard than everyone else. Example: *I don't mind if your desk is a mess, but I keep mine neat and tidy.*
Catastrophizing	You expect the worst. Example: *I was late on the rent. I'm going to be evicted.*
Labeling	You label yourself negatively. Example: *I made a mistake. I'm a failure.*
Magical thinking	You think everything will be better when _____ (you're thinner, smarter, or richer; you get a new job). Example: *I'll meet Mr. Right once I lose twenty pounds.*
Should Statements	You judge yourself and criticize yourself for what you should be doing. Example: *I should run five miles every day before work.*

Appendix B

Questions for Challenging Perfectionist Thinking

- How do I know if this thought is accurate?

- What evidence do I have to support this thought or belief?

- Do I have a trusted friend whom I can check out these thoughts with?

- Is this thought helpful?

- Are there other ways that I can think of this situation or myself?

- Am I blaming myself unnecessarily?

- What or who else contributed to this situation?

- Is it really in my control?

- Am I overgeneralizing?

- Am I making assumptions?

- What would I say to a friend in this situation?

- Can I look for shades of gray?

- Am I assuming the worst?

- Am I holding myself to an unreasonable or double standard?

- Are there exceptions to these absolutes (always, never)?

- Am I making this personal when it isn't?

- Who gets to decide what I have to or should do?

- Does this align with my values?

- Is this a realistic expectation?

- Am I expecting myself to be perfect?

Appendix C

Feeling Words

Positive Feelings

- calm
- peaceful
- at ease
- comfortable
- pleased
- encouraged
- clever
- surprised
- content
- quiet
- certain
- relaxed
- serene
- blessed
- reassured
- good
- strong
- secure
- impulsive
- free
- sure

- great
- fortunate
- rebellious
- bold
- anxious
- glad
- joyful
- playful
- courageous
- energetic
- optimistic
- provocative
- frisky
- animated
- spirited
- thrilled
- wonderful
- alive
- positive
- eager
- keen

- unique
- loved
- comforted
- thankful
- important
- festive
- understanding
- confident
- reliable
- amazed
- sympathetic
- interested
- satisfied
- receptive
- accepting
- kind
- happy
- loving
- considerate
- affectionate
- sensitive

- devoted
- attracted
- passionate
- admiration
- warm
- ecstatic
- lucky
- curious
- concerned
- inquisitive
- inspired
- determined
- excited
- enthusiastic
- elated
- cheerful
- touched
- challenged
- hopeful
- intrigued
- brave

Uncomfortable Feelings

- angry
- helpless
- incapable
- alone
- paralyzed
- fatigued
- useless
- inferior
- vulnerable
- empty
- hesitant
- despair
- frustrated
- distressed
- pathetic
- hurt
- crushed
- tormented
- confused
- upset
- uncertain
- embarrassed

- shy
- disillusioned
- skeptical
- distrustful
- lost
- unsure
- uneasy
- pessimistic
- victimized
- heartbroken
- appalled
- humiliated
- wronged
- alienated
- indifferent
- unhappy
- lonely
- threatened
- deprived
- pained
- rejected
- offended

- reserved
- bored
- depressed
- lousy
- disappointed
- discouraged
- ashamed
- powerless
- guilty
- dissatisfied
- miserable
- disgusting
- terrible
- tense
- sad
- tearful
- sorrowful
- irritated
- enraged
- hostile
- annoyed
- hateful

- offensive
- bitter
- aggressive
- resentful
- preoccupied
- cold
- provoked
- infuriated
- indignant
- afraid
- fearful
- terrified
- suspicious
- anxious
- scared
- worried
- desperate
- panic
- nervous
- restless
- shaky

Appendix D

Self-Care Activities

- Sit outside and enjoy nature
- Have coffee with a friend
- Do a guided meditation
- Watch the sunrise or sunset
- Journal
- Color
- Read a good book
- Knit or crochet
- Listen to a podcast
- Take a nap
- Practice deep breathing
- Call a friend
- Take a vacation day
- Walk along the ocean
- Blow bubbles
- Pet your cat or dog

- Take yourself out to lunch
- Doodle
- Cuddle with your partner
- Speak up for yourself
- Take a real lunch break during the workday
- Go to a religious service
- Go to bed on time
- Write yourself a love letter
- Do a crossword puzzle
- Go to the library
- Have a snack
- Do just one thing at a time
- Take photos
- Sit in silence and do nothing
- Reread a favorite book from childhood
- Feed the ducks

- Say no to something you don't want to do

- Stargaze

- Take a class because you want to

- Have a family game night

- Take a bubble bath

- Pray

- Talk to a therapist

- Take medication as prescribed

- Eat a healthy meal

- Pick flowers in your garden

- Crank up the music and sing along

- Practice yoga

- Watch a funny YouTube video

- Play the piano, guitar, or another instrument

- Dance

- Bike ride

- Light a scented candle or diffuse essential oils

- Play with your dog

- Hike

- Pull weeds in your garden or water your plants

- Make something

- _____

- _____

- _____

- _____

- _____

- _____

- _____

- _____

- _____

References

Aron, E. N. 1998. *The Highly Sensitive Person: How to Thrive When the World Overwhelms You*. New York: Harmony Books.

Aron, E. N. 2004. "Comfort Zone" (newsletter). *The Highly Sensitive Person*, http://www.hsper son.com/pages/edAug04.htm.

Brown, B. 2012. *Daring Greatly: How the Courage to Be Vulnerable Transforms the Way We Live, Love, Parent, and Lead*. New York: Gotham.

Chua, A. 2011. *Battle Hymn of the Tiger Mother*. London: Bloomsbury.

Emmons, R. A., and M. E. McCullough. 2003. "Counting Blessings Versus Burdens: An Experimental Investigation of Gratitude and Subjective Well-Being in Daily Life." *Journal of Personality and Social Psychology* 84, no. 2: 377–89.

Gottman, J., and N. Silver. 2015. *The Seven Principles for Making Marriage Work: A Practical Guide from the Country's Foremost Relationship Expert*. New York: Harmony Books.

Hewitt, P. L., and G. L. Flett. 1991. "Perfectionism in the Self and Social Contexts: Conceptualization, Assessment, and Association with Psychopathology." *Journal of Personality and Social Psychology* 60, no. 3: 456–70.

Hewitt, P. L., G. L. Flett, and S. F. Mikail. 2017. *Perfectionism: A Relational Approach to Conceptualization, Assessment, and Treatment*. New York: Guilford Press.

Lowes, J., and M. Tiggemann. 2003. "Body Dissatisfaction, Dieting Awareness and the Impact of Parental Influence in Young Children." *The British Journal of Health Psychology* 8: 135–47.

Neff, K. 2011. *Self-Compassion: The Proven Power of Being Kind to Yourself*. New York: HarperCollins.

Pai, S., and K. Schryver. 2015. *Children, Teens, Media, and Body Image*. San Francisco: Common Sense Media.

Seligman, M. E. P., T. A. Steen, N. Park, and C. Peterson. 2005. "Positive Psychology Progress: Empirical Validation of Interventions." *American Psychologist* 60, no. 5: 410–21.

Sharon Martin, MSW, LCSW, is a psychotherapist, writer, speaker, and media contributor on emotional health and relationships. Her psychotherapy practice in San Jose, CA, specializes in helping individuals overcome codependency and perfectionism, and learn to accept and love themselves.

Foreword writer **Julie de Azevedo Hanks, PhD, LCSW,** is a psychotherapist, licensed clinical social worker, author of *The Burnout Cure* and *The Assertiveness Guide for Women*, and founder and director of Wasatch Family Therapy.

Real change *is* possible

For more than fifty years, New Harbinger has published proven-effective self-help books and pioneering workbooks to help readers of all ages and backgrounds improve mental health and well-being, and achieve lasting personal growth. In addition, our spirituality books offer profound guidance for deepening awareness and cultivating healing, self-discovery, and fulfillment.

Founded by psychologist Matthew McKay and Patrick Fanning, New Harbinger is proud to be an independent, employee-owned company. Our books reflect our core values of integrity, innovation, commitment, sustainability, compassion, and trust. Written by leaders in the field and recommended by therapists worldwide, New Harbinger books are practical, accessible, and provide real tools for real change.

 **newharbinger**publications

MORE BOOKS *from*
NEW HARBINGER PUBLICATIONS

Did you know there are **free tools** you can download for this book?

Free tools are things like **worksheets**, **guided meditation exercises**, and **more** that will help you get the most out of your book.

You can download free tools for this book—whether you bought or borrowed it, in any format, from any source—from the New Harbinger website. All you need is a NewHarbinger.com account. Just use the URL provided in this book to view the free tools that are available for it. Then, click on the "download" button for the free tool you want, and follow the prompts that appear to log in to your NewHarbinger.com account and download the material.

You can also save the free tools for this book to your **Free Tools Library** so you can access them again anytime, just by logging in to your account! Just look for this button on the book's free tools page.

+ Save this to my free tools library

If you need help accessing or downloading free tools, visit **newharbinger.com/faq** or contact us at **customerservice@newharbinger.com**.